A million moments of Love
Sensuous Glorification of Romance

FRANK CHUKWUDUBEM AMOBI
FAMOBY POETRY ©

A MILLION MOMENTS OF LOVE

Copyright © 2021 by FRANK C. AMOBI

All rights reserved. No part of this book may be reproduced, stored in a retrieval system, or transmitted in any form or by any means, electronic, mechanical, photocopying, recording, or otherwise, without the prior written permission of the author, except as provided by U.S.A. copyright law.

The Publisher does not have any control over and does not assume any responsibility for author or third-party websites or their content.

ISBN:
Print: 978-1-952744-04-4
Ebook: 978-1-952744-20-4

WGA: 1339863

Edited by: Nkem DenChukwu

Published By:
Eleviv Publishing Group
www.elevivpublishing.com

Published and Printed in the United States of America

10 9 8 7 6 5 4 3 2

To my wife, Cherly; thank you for your love. With all my love.

To my son, Brinton, and his wife, Dylan, I love you both.

To my granddaughter, Chimdi Brinn Zulena; for bringing new joy and laughter in our lives. I love you.

To the entire Amobi family and my friends; Your love and support mean the world to me.

Preface

While the earth revolves, natural events evolve, hence, the human mind travels along. As you read this lyrical collection of love poems, passion, and romance, keep an open mind, and see yourself as you are or were loved, or imagine to be loved.

I was born in the beautiful, mountainous, cold region of Northern Nigeria; Plateau State capital city of Jos. It lies on the Delimi River and near the source of the Jamaari River called the Bunga. But, growing up in a natural valley of the village of Obosi in the Southeast Nigeria, I really loved, and appreciated its tropical surroundings. I love the authenticity that both possess.

I believe the passion for my musing and organic writings were inspired by the forces of Nature and its surroundings in synchronization with my beautiful childhood experiences. Writing this collection; my first collection, came out of deep meditative and imaginative raw thoughts about love, romance, life, and realistic human struggles over the unending need and yearnings for love and passion.
I hope you will enjoy reading this collection as much as I loved writing it.

Frank C. Amobi

Life is nothing without a compromise
Your heart decides whom to love
But your mind holds you back
Let go of your mind
Love with no expectations
Then, accept love.

Table of Contents

The Eve's of God's Creation..1

Let me love you babe (Lyric)..2

Baby, it's Midnight (Sensuously Rated)..5

The God of Love Life..7

Let me Shower, Babe (Sensuously Rated)..9

Tell me a Story (Lyric)...11

Hibiscus and Roses (Lyric)..13

Where are you?...16

Night Love for Breakfast...19

When you Sleep..21

My Ocean Pearl (Lyric)...23

It Just Feels Right (Lyric)..26

My Heart...Your Heart...29

I Have Seen Her Before...32

Breadfruit of the Night (Sensuously Rated)...35

Deep down in my Mind (Lyrics)...37

My Butterfly Girl (Lyric)..40

The Light is Out, Baby (Sensuously Rated)..43

Nothing Beyond Nothing (Ida) (Lyric)...45

The Village Night Secrets...47

The Way I Love (Sensuously Rated)..49

Let's Do the Dance (Lyric)...52

Where are you? (Lyric)...55

Don't Cry (Lyric) 58
You Missed Me 60
You Fill My Intimate Pleasures (Sensuously Rated) 63
Waiting for her (Lyric)(Sensuously Rated) 65
You Loved too Much 68
Leave me not alone (Lyric) 71
Please Love Again 74
Down the Trail with Bae 76
Natural Beauty You (Lyric) 78
My Life a Music (Lyric) 80
Looking Back 83
Reserve your Strength for the Day (Lyric) 85
The Things you Admire (Lyric) 87
Let the Flamingos Fly (Lyric) 89
The Mind of Orlando (Lyric) 92
I don't see color (Lyric) 95
The Silent Whispers of the Great Blue Heron 98
A Cry Answered (A Tribute to Oprah) 101
This Sunday Morning 104
The Mid-Day Darkness 107
Without a Grudge 110
You Think You're Tired 112
Here I Am 114
Frank's Life Quotes 116

The Eve's of God's Creation

The words!
The voices of the gods;
The gods of Nature
The nature of our minds: Our minds?
The passionate reveal of earthly realities in practice
Sometimes gentle
Most times brutal
Yet, the God of creations insists the gentle spoken
Now, the words are spoken
The gentle words
The recipients?
The Eves of God's creations
Our mothers, your mothers, their mothers
The entire women of humanity
In whom all human should adore
In whom all beings should please more
In whom all things should bow before
In whom the earth goddesses are cheering for
In whom the Supreme Being; the God of creations, leaves no regrets
In whom the calmness of our earth shares responsibility
In whom all humanity dares not forget
The mothers, the Eves of Supreme creations
The reasons of earthly tranquility and peace
The peace of our minds
The ones we hold dearer to God.

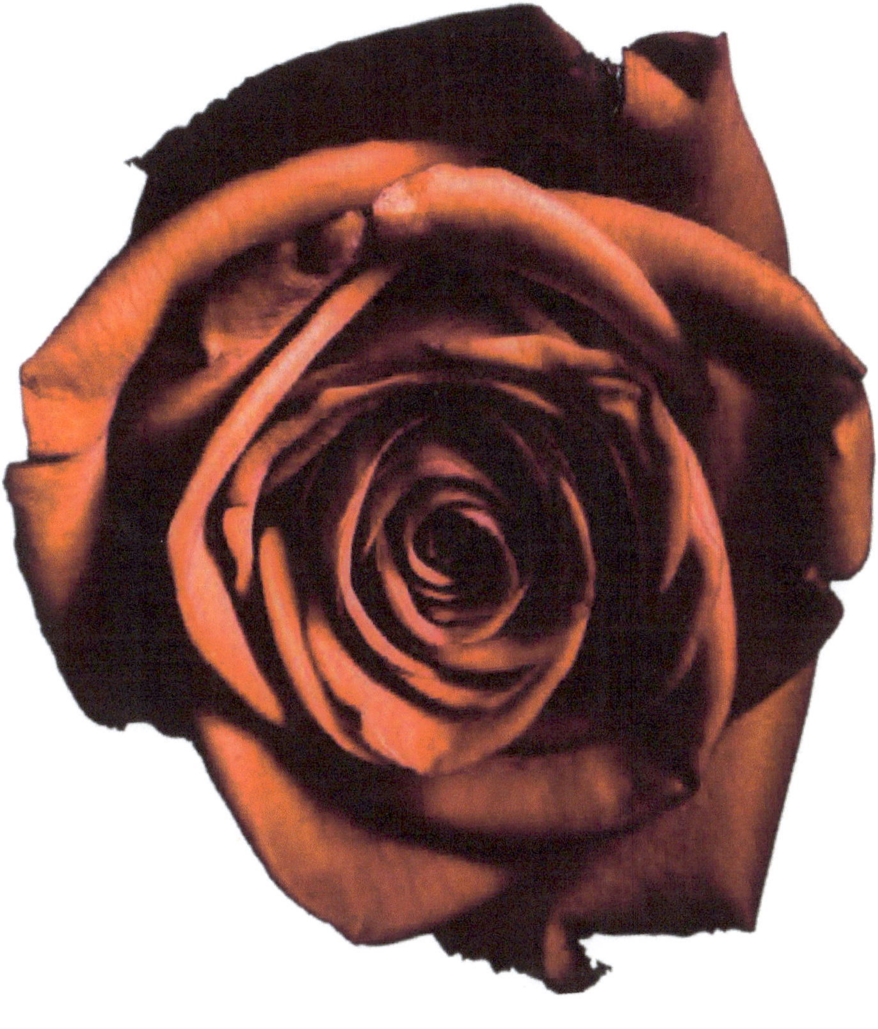

Let me love you babe (Lyric)

Give me a minute, Babe
I will return to claim you
Remember our promise
We never get over our passionate charms
We can always recall our beginning love rhythms
In our real world we cry alone
What can I do to get our glory back?
I still yearn for our day in moonlight to come back
Let me love you again, Babe

Since you disappeared from my shadows
I feel the pain of empty separation
I tried and pretended not to show it
The look on your face lets me know you are hurt
I am hurt for your heart
Come to me to read your heart
Your kind-heartfelt proposal warms my earth
I should have known better not to forget
Let me love you again, Babe

Allow my proposal into your world again
I throw my arrows of love to hit your sensitive balance
I will not miss the target this time for substance
It will make sense for the last time
Again, you will melt in my sensual resolve
Come lead me to welcome you
Let me love you again, Babe

(CHORUS)
Say you love me again to my heart
I say I love you again in my heart
Let me love you again, Babe

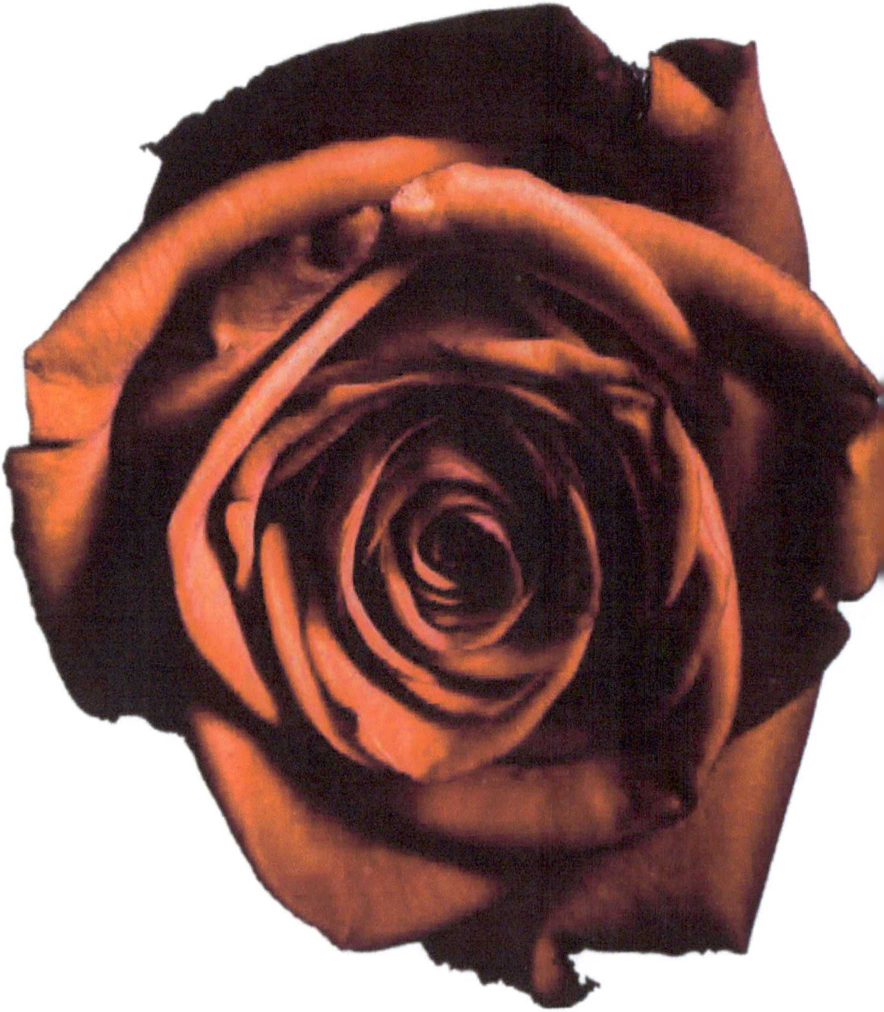

Baby, it's Midnight
(Sensuously Rated)

Hello baby, it's me
I'm about to put some plans into action
All day I scheme and ponder, yet wonder
Here now, the air in my corner is your nightly
aroma in motion
In my naughty senses, I dwell on my plan of wonders
Looking at the clock, I waist no time
Waiting for Friday night to strike twelve midnight
The face of the moon tells me it's time
So, let me pour your red wine

That fresh scent of your after-shower;
Already my preparation is too easy, but I'm fine
Now, all that I see here is pure sweetness;
A taste of honey might not compare
Feelings I receive revive the sound of the owl tonight
It makes much sense now;
We are ready to pair
As I see the dark shadows of the midnight
under the moonlight.

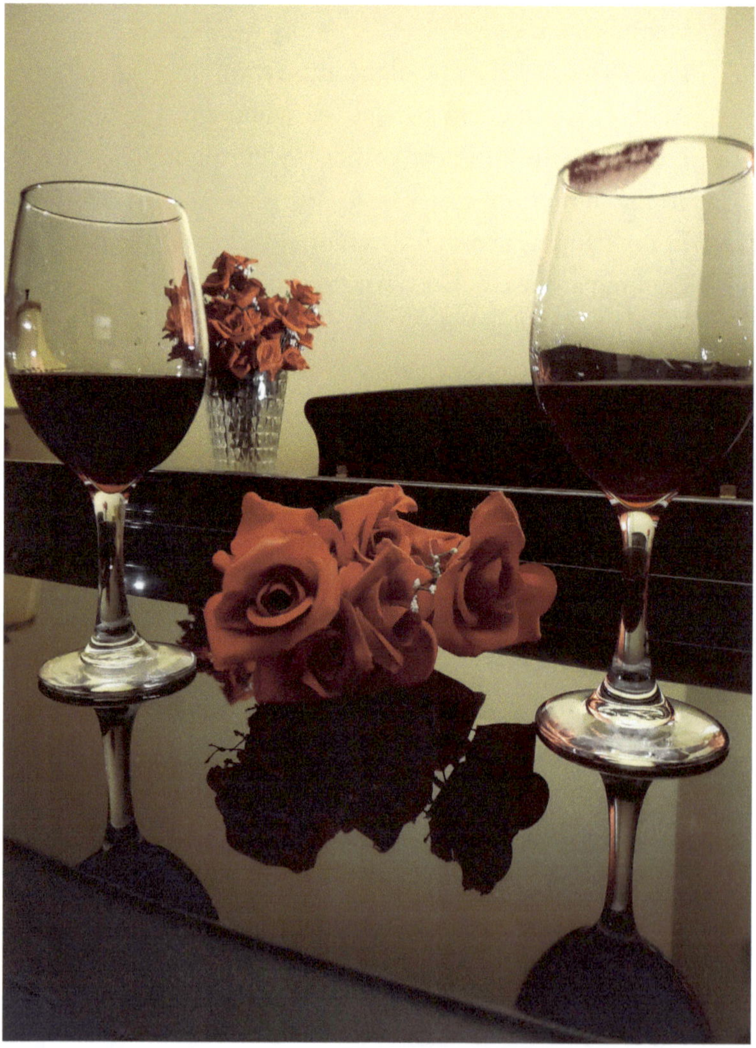

The God of Love Life

One mind, one heart; a bit closer
Never had the sound of heartbeat same
Distant separation too close
We feel too near and choose
Nearness that brings glue to the fight
Two lovers glued together in mind
Where is the God of love to find?

How did He find this and fight?
A fight for me to win this time
A chance that matched me up with my love for life
We share anything
We remember everything
We say many things
We refuse most things
Most of them we allow ourselves to do…naughty things

Now we can laugh, even together apart
While we hear ourselves often in silence
We imagine the precious blue sky that we created together
The God of Love, you did well this time around altogether.

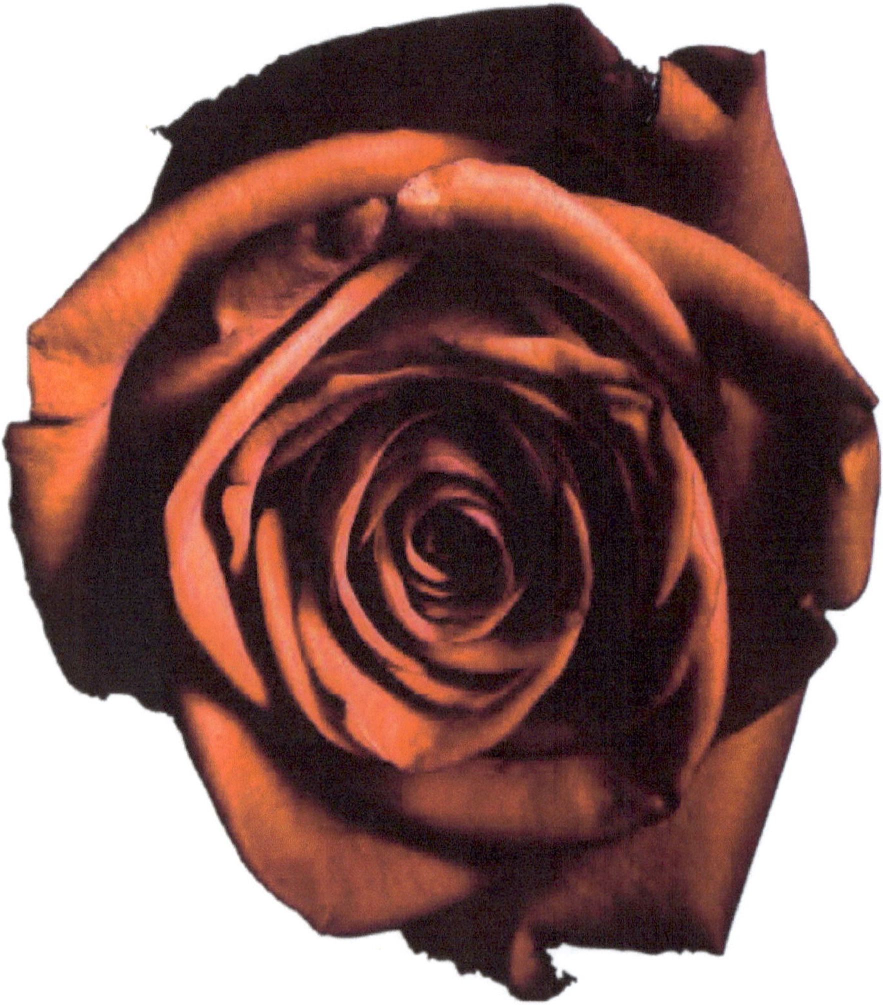

Let me Shower, Babe

O' my goodness!
That word;
Eruption of feelings, a mounting in flame to color
I like to watch her glamour
She just arrived, a hot summer in my favor
Outside, the sunflower answers to the sun
Inside my sumptuous jacuzzi, welcomes her fun
As her sweet fragrance merges in the steaming, bubbling water

My sense of taste and smell comes alive and well
I prepared the white chocolate in cream as well
To suit the ice cream that soothes her palate
Strawberries in my hands as she appeared fresh and wet
She kissed me as I intend to boost her libido
Gently, she accepts my fingers to feed her soft tongue

I imagined otherwise, not my finger to soften
"Dry me, babe," a word I waited and dreamt of often
My black leather couch could bear witness
I am soaking wet in natural cream of kindness
We rolled and rolled in tangle like Twizzlers candy
We are now sweeter, twisted and tastier
Just because my babe took a shower.

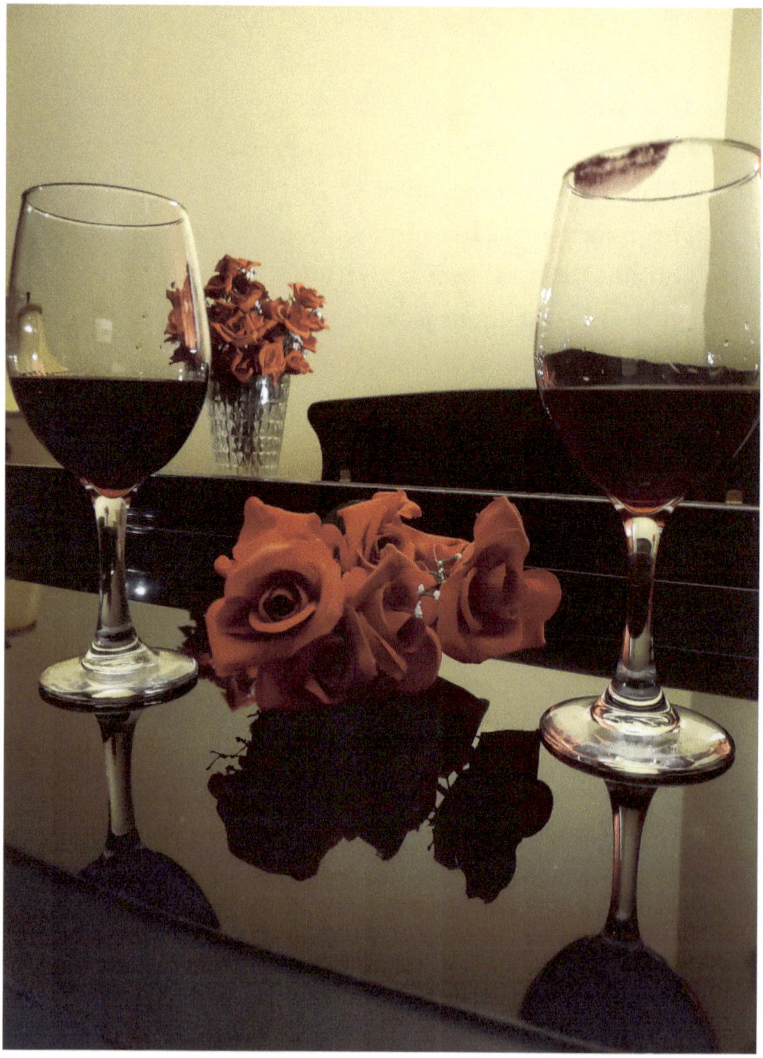

Tell me a Story (Lyric)

Tell me a story;
A story of love to remember
The whispers of your voice when you lay close to me
The aroma of chocolate scent fills the room
The closer you get to me;
The powerful sensation of my nature is reviving
The closer you are to me babe;
The deeper I feel the tense of my muscles jumping
The heat of your closeness babe;
The making of warm chocolate melt

Your embrace… Oh! Sweet, sweet feelings of your warm soul
Your embrace… Oh! So sweet my anticipation of our merging souls

Your dreams and my dreams sent chills down my spine
Your mellow voice gives me the feelings that
I cannot take back
Your firm possessions now I can call mine
Tell me a story of love that came back
While you feel my pounding heart
Lead my nature to victory;
While we move the heavens and the earth
Babe, tell me a love story over and over again.

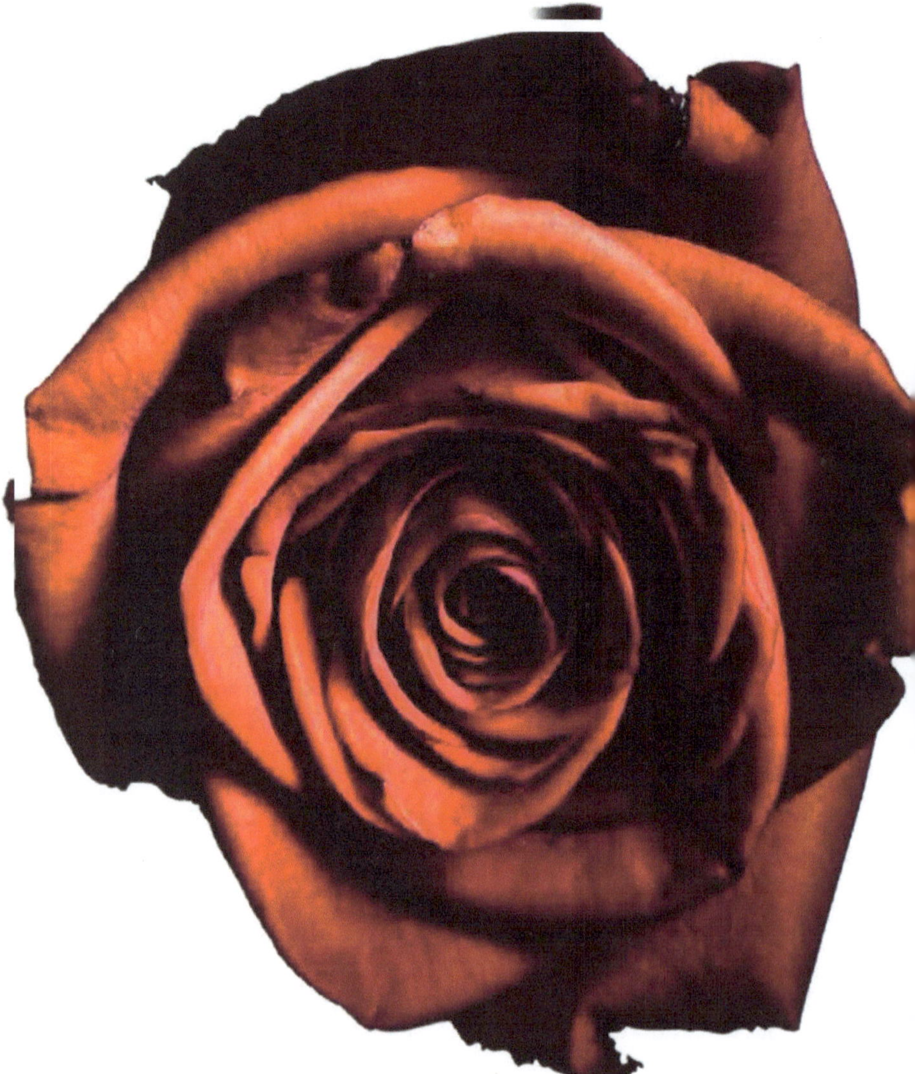

Hibiscus and Roses (Lyric)

You revealed to me the colors of the stars
Under the moonlight shadows;
I can see the flares your eyes reveal
The colors of stars I see on your face
Same colors of the Hibiscus and Roses in the vase
Watching the flowers at sunset reminds me
of your blooming reveal
Remember we use to chase each other around a flowerbed?
Remember how you let me catch you on the bed we made?

Again, let me catch you for a while
Again, let me see that sweet smile;
Same smile that welcomes my gentle caress
Again, let my lips be my only witness
Ooh! That kiss.

The sunset always brings us the colors of the flowers
Your short dresses always match the colors of the summer
Like Hibiscus and Roses; you blossom with every summer's call
We were young always in the summer
Our minds would not tell us the meanings
of the summer colors
Now, we know the colors we see are the colors of love.

Fill me with the love you feel
I can feel the same love you feel
Now, our minds can tell the love we feel

Let us write our childhood memories in many words
Our words will reveal the steam of passion we feel
Let our promises come through to each and every word
We will dance around in the woods for the spring leaves
While the petals of Hibiscus flowers and Roses tell the stories
The stories of a match made from our young curious discoveries.

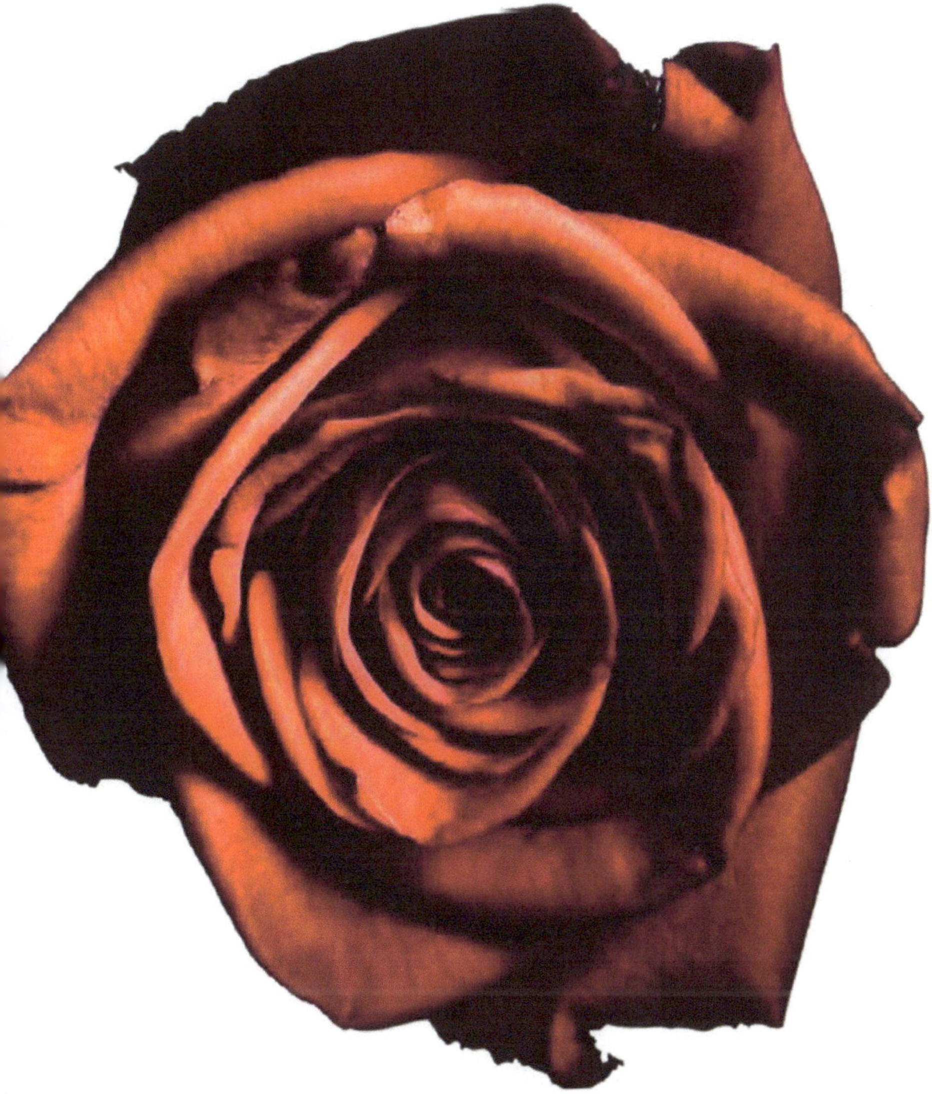

Where are you?

Last night, I started my search;
A search that would lead me to wonder
In my mind, the questions left me to ponder
Is this it?

The flashing memories of your last smile
Your last word to me, "I'll be fine"
Here in my small world;
I try to answer my own questions
You left my affection stranded in mid air;
Battered with inflictions
Like a Lone Ranger, I tried to be strong
Sometimes I wonder the state of my turmoil
What could I have done wrong?
In my states of solitude and soliloquy;
Is anyone listening?
Or, is this it?

Your last word kept coming back to me
Yet, an uncertain reflection clouds my sweet expectation
Will I be here to find you?
I'll seize the opportunity, and what a sweet anticipation
You told me everything about so much
Why do you become the sole possessor of my heart and soul?
Only to fly away with so much
Still I wonder, while I listen to the silent
echoes of my yearnings

My deep breathing interfering with the empty
sound of the presence
Again, in my states of solitude and soliloquy
Is anyone listening?
Or, is this it?

In my dreams, I fly around the dark misty night
My eyes dashing side-to-side like a hawk in search of a prey
Only this time, my search found a glare;
Piercing through the darkness of the night; your eyes
The welcoming dimples of your smile
But once again, in my states of solitude and soliloquy
Is anyone listening?
Or, is this it?

Suddenly, a voice sneaks through the dark clouds
The silence is broken and my eyes recover
Here you are, wrapped around my flying wings, in my arms
Again, I heard; "I'm right here, babe. I'm right here."

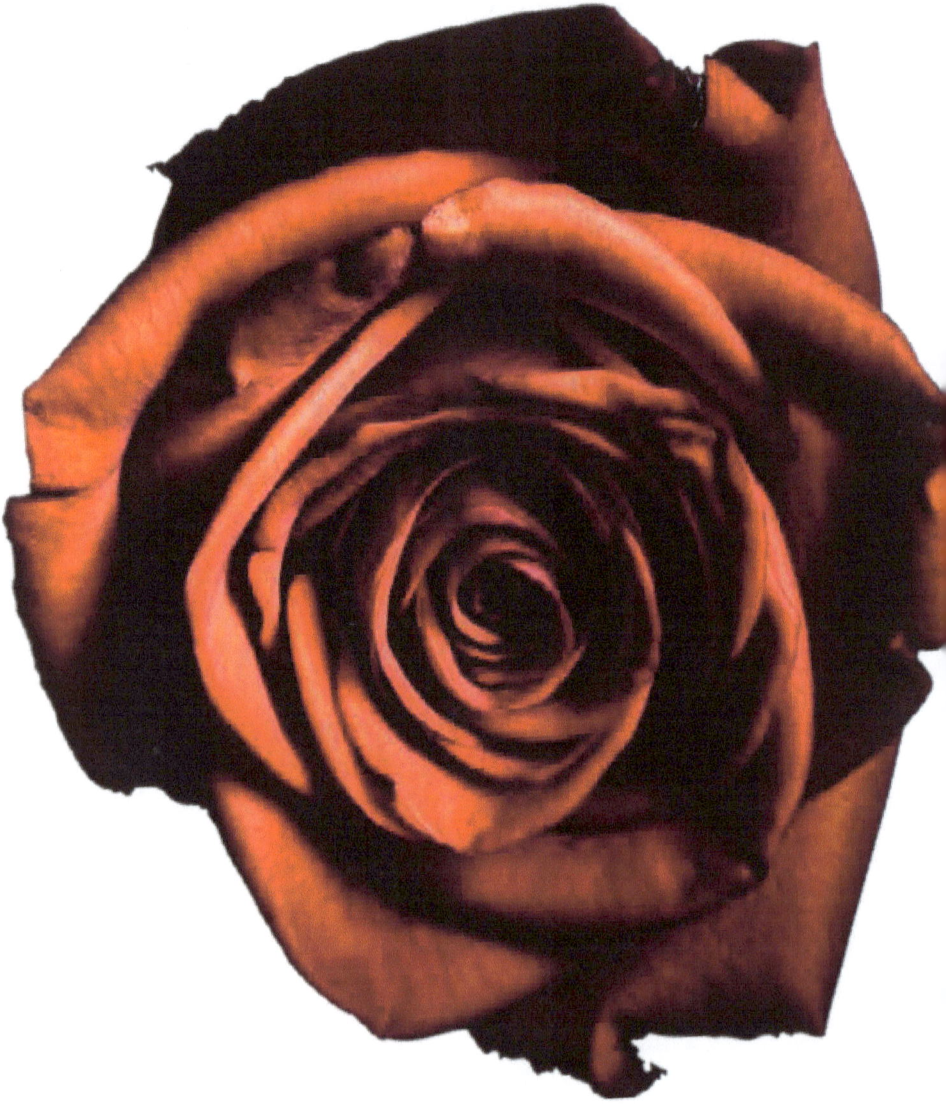

Night Love for Breakfast

Six chicken eggs to fry
The morning after a love fairy
What we are made of after a night
that felt like Nightingales party
Six eggs, succulent of pleasure
How the yellow-melted yolks glow in the balcony
Dripping down to suit the yellow morning sunflower
Yes, six eggs we ate in silent gaze at each other
As we feel the joy of laughter

Six eggs that two lovers share
A morning toast and crunchy bread crumbs
all over the marble floor
Reminding the little village ants breakfast is free for share
Six eggs, six smudge lines on the white napkin
A colorful evidence of an instant wet kiss
The doses that sold me late night to my darling
Here again in the morning;
We remember our fate over six eggs and a kiss.

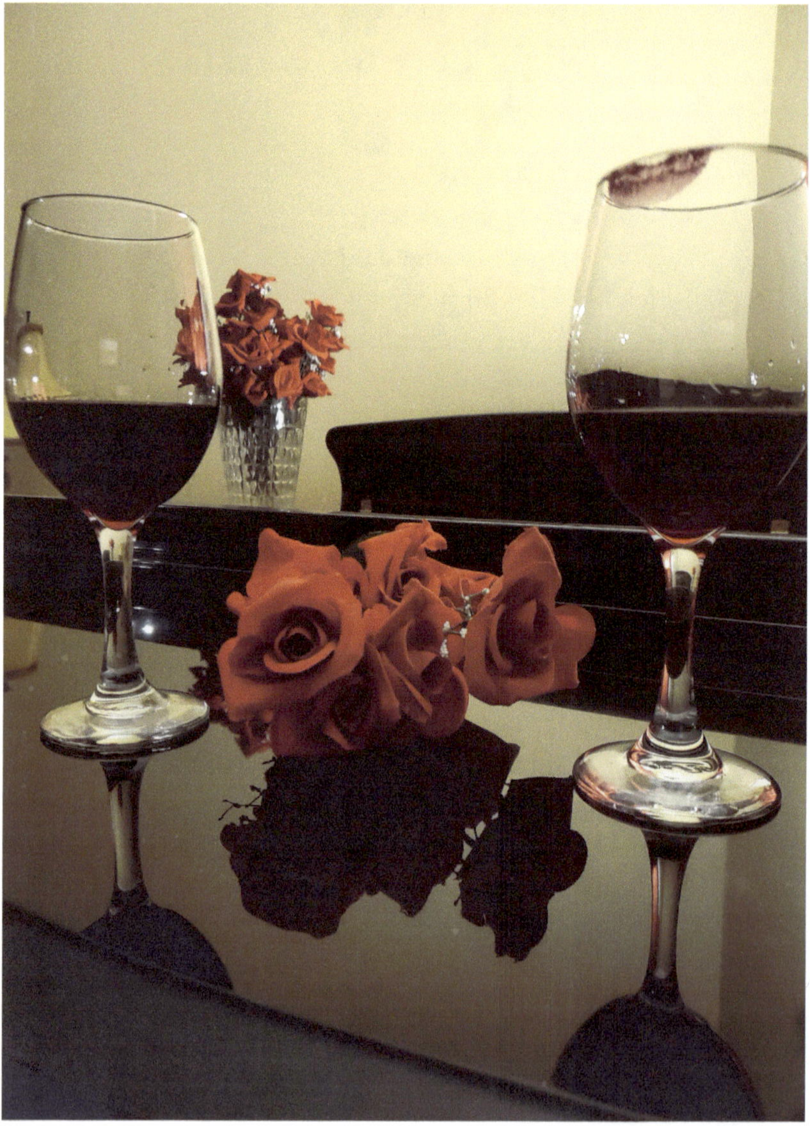

When you Sleep

The morning without me;
It's a morning I didn't ask for
But, today away from you is not what I proposed
As I listen to the birds outside call for morning mating
Here I starve to watch you dance in the morning sunshine

The colorful autumn leaves fall without a plan
of smooth landing
Yet, the Nature offer of hand for their capture is fair
I lay flat with open hands in the air
I received these dropping leaves of the fall
to accept your dream
I watched you sleep last night, like a
child expecting ice cream

I stayed awake watching you sleep
Sleep evaded me as passion slowly creeps
Slowly a mischievous act in mind
I am in complex mix feelings to wake you

Here, my princess lays next to me
The freshness of your breath calls for my kiss
I intend to wake you to calm me
A satisfaction that will confirm our bliss
Yes, I want to wake you, babe.

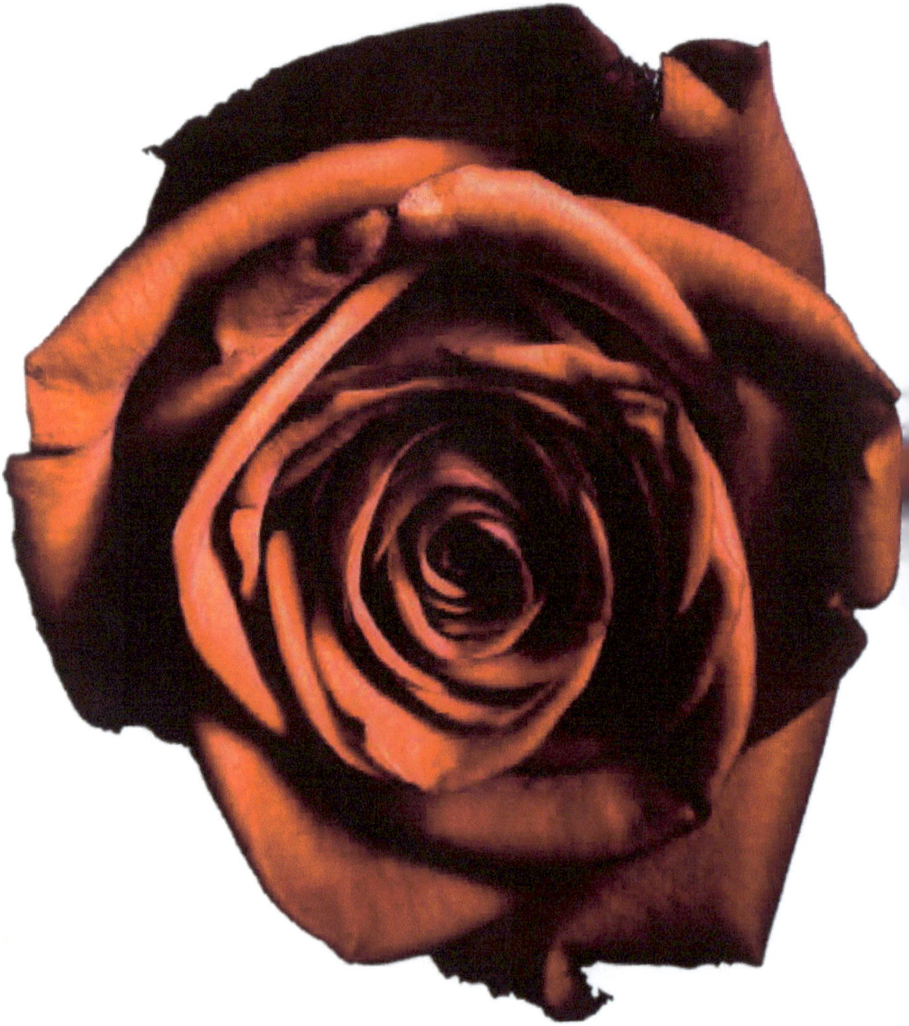

My Ocean Pearl (Lyric)

Give me your heart that I discovered
Replace my feelings with the one I found
You prepared my heart for the one I recovered
So, save me your heart that I found
For the one in me will be the one you hold
Leave me your heart of silver and gold
While I prepare to receive the rhythm of your soul
I'll promise to lift your mind up to the skylights above
Then you'll see in me what my heart says I hold
For that, I say; 'You are my ocean pearl.'

The love I possessed deep inside of me;
I long to give them all back to you
Even only a gentle caress from me to you;
Shows me the true epiphany of your love that I seek
I see in you what my heart says I'll do for you
I'll say to you, 'Wear these gemstones made for you'
I'll imagine your body covered in diamond necklaces;
Wrapped around and draped down
on your smooth skin to fit;
Your shimmering body like an Egyptian goddess
For that, I say; 'You are my ocean pearl.'
You put me in the zone over the ocean
I watched the silent approach of your reflection
As you stroll down to me in slow motion
The way you float on the walk, a sign of perfection
As in smooth jazz music on a midnight rhapsody

I am in the zone for sure
Here now, you are succulent like candy
I will call you my ornaments for sure
You'll be my complete package that says,
'Fragile! Handle With Care' just like an ocean pearl
Oh yes! You are my ocean pearl.

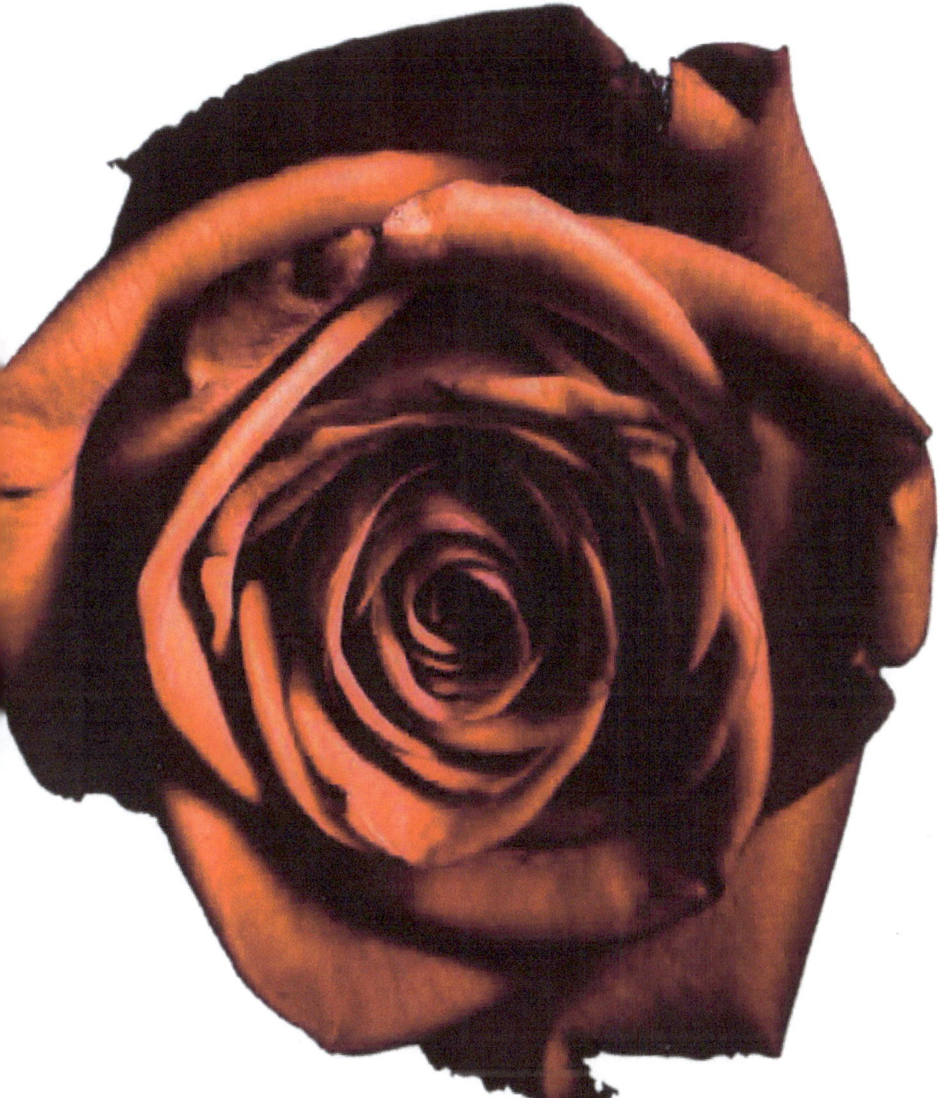

It Just Feels Right (Lyric)

I am here now
I am here now for you
Take my warm hands, honey
As you cried out for me
You seem so far, yet so close to me
In silence alone in darkness;
I see the clouds that blind my vision
My recollection tells me you need my closeness
Then a taste of your love potion
Here, I seem to awaken;
Because it just feels right.

What ever feels right;
Is a good thing
Doing the right thing;
Is a good thing
Is just feels too right to deserve you
Heaven better know;
You deserve the best of love
Heaven better know;
You need my warm hands
Heaven better know;
Your tear drops left a spot close to my heart.

Baby, take my warm hands
For too long, your beauty stays ignored
For too long, your silent cries undiscovered

For too long in silence, you called on me
Here now with you, your soul is what I feel
Now I lend my hands to dry your tears
Now I reach over the wall to pull you closer to me
I look up to the blue sky
The clouds of passion seem clearer to me
Whatever brought me you, who am I to ask why?
Just to say, something feels too right.
(CHORUS)

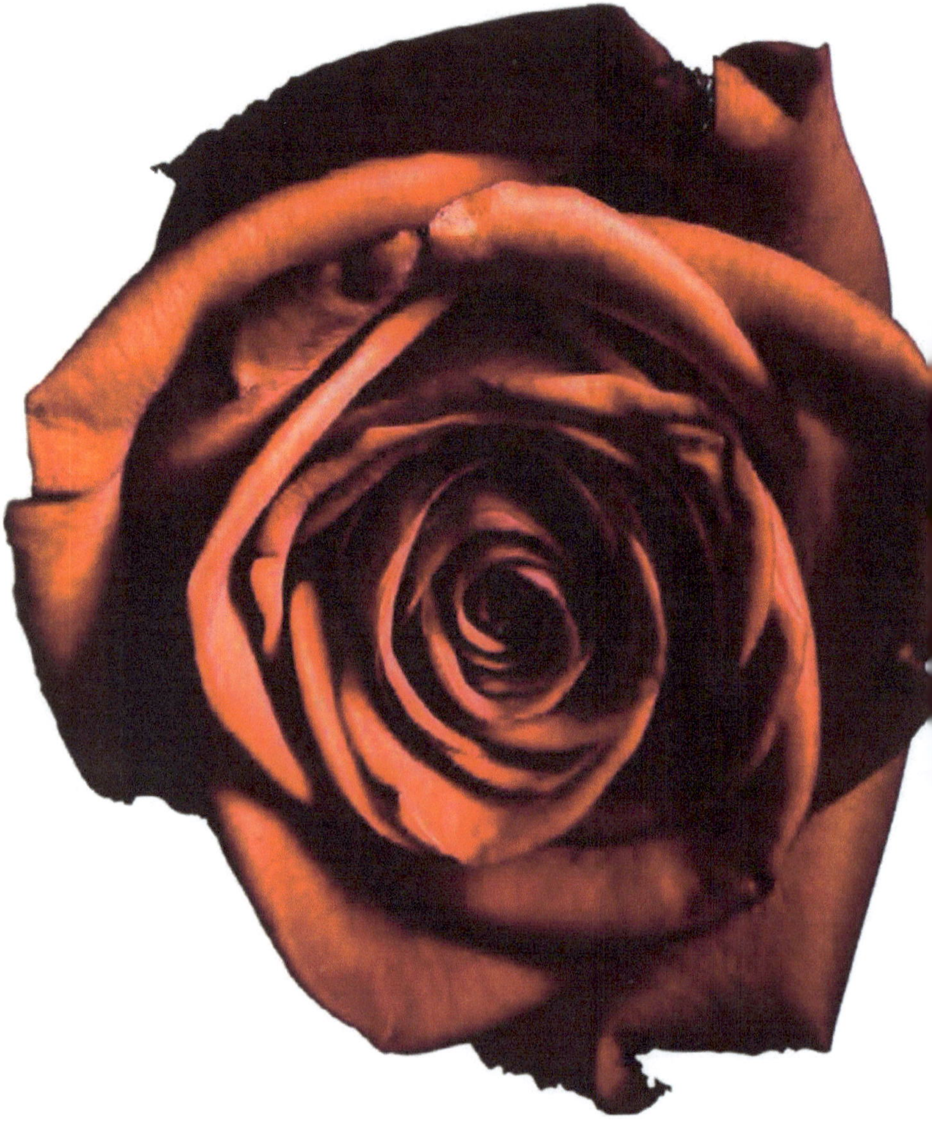

My Heart...Your Heart

The heart; the heartbeats
Life; the life from your beats
You gave us existence
You gave us emotions
You gave us persistence
Yes, we must fight for generations to come
Our children will see our fights outcome
The desires we share with life
Same desires for our children remain in sight

Our hearts, love of life so bright
Yes, you lead us in solidarity
We must refuse to live in mediocrity
Heart; you are the life manager
Our great senses of revival yet to conclude
We envelope the gifts of life
As our blood pump into your chambers

Heart, your confidence resolve gives us life
Heart, through you, we give and take love
Through you, we cry
Through you, we grief
Through you, we pray

Heart, in you we share
In you we fare
In you we desire

In you we admire
In you we cherish
In you we are promised;
A promise that we stay confident in life and love.

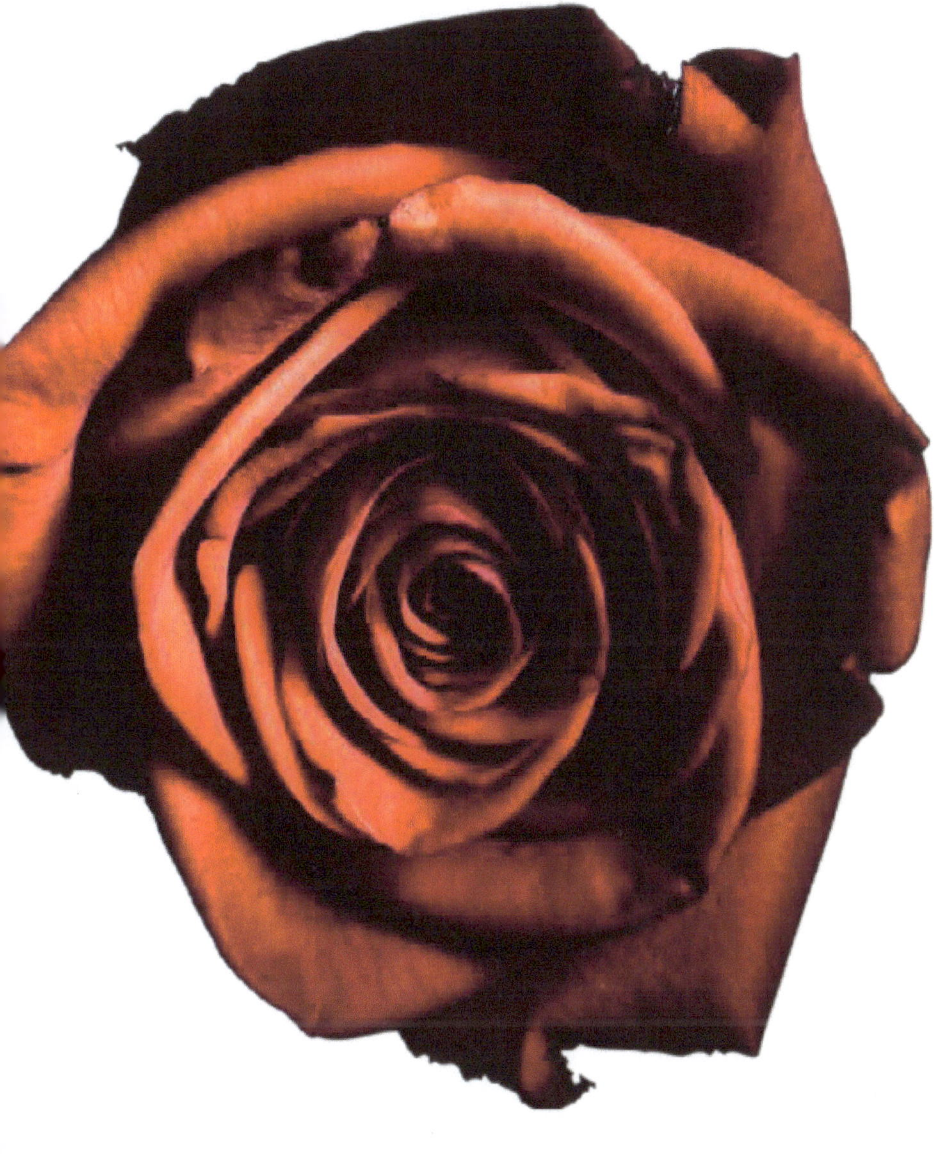

I Have Seen Her Before

"Hi…" That's it…that was all she said
CLICK…There she is;
"Hi," I said
I have seen her before
No; Not in person
Those eyes, that nose, the smile with all the reasons;
I have seen this face before
As I starred at her picture;
I tried to make sense of my imaginations
I asked myself, 'Should I proceed without limitations?'

Then, her voice came through the line;
The voice that grabbed my attention
I heard the sound of my name so divine
A sweet sound of wind chimes
The soothing voice, a reminder of my masculinity
The smoothest tone of femininity
She spoke with a sense of tease
A fascinating tendency is felt with ease;
Yet, speculative of something good for late night

As she spoke, her joviality was just right
A tantalizing reminder of a late-night adult bed play
As she spoke, she mentioned her loves;
CLICK…Here they are, the three boys
They made her the Mother that she is
Wow! How beautiful in all appearances

Yet, she retains her quiet youthful exuberance
I know now that I have seen her before.

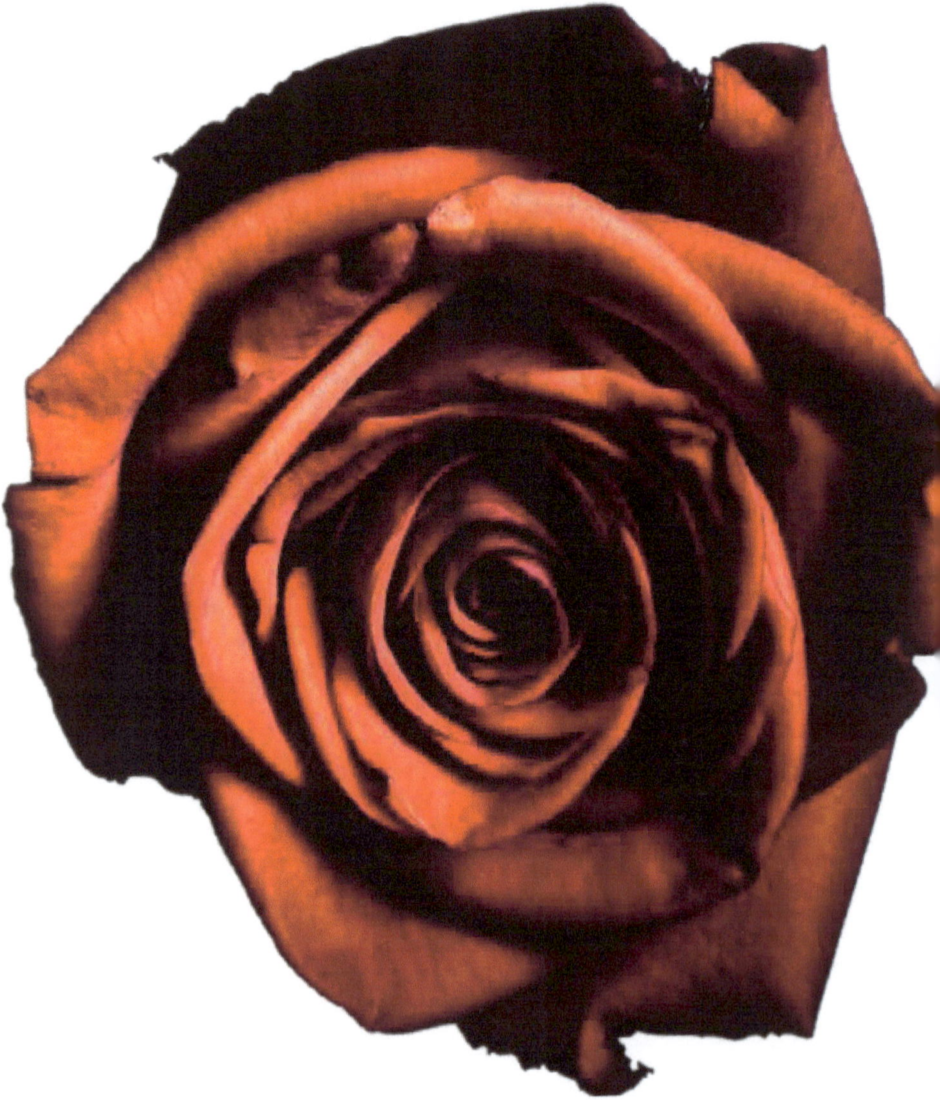

Breadfruit of the Night
(Sensuously Rated)

Breadfruit of the night;
Prepared for the delicious night
We ate the dish of flavor earth dessert
Sucking our fingers for tasteful enjoyment
You fed me, I fed you, and I felt your natural cream
I kissed you; you kissed me like a dream

The dish served in passion tray
Look, the bed is stained by our play
Why were we so much in love?
We listened to the songs of the doves
Outside our window, the doves ignored our presence

While the doves were dancing, we danced with Nature in bed
Oh… those fingers got wet again
I said, "Let me lick for a taste that you made"
Oh…your fingers were blessed for my gain

I am in my mood again
Your playful gestures are doing it to me for fulfillment
Your body so warm, my skin in hot amazement
Let me love you, while we feast on the breadfruit of life
Oh…so delicious!

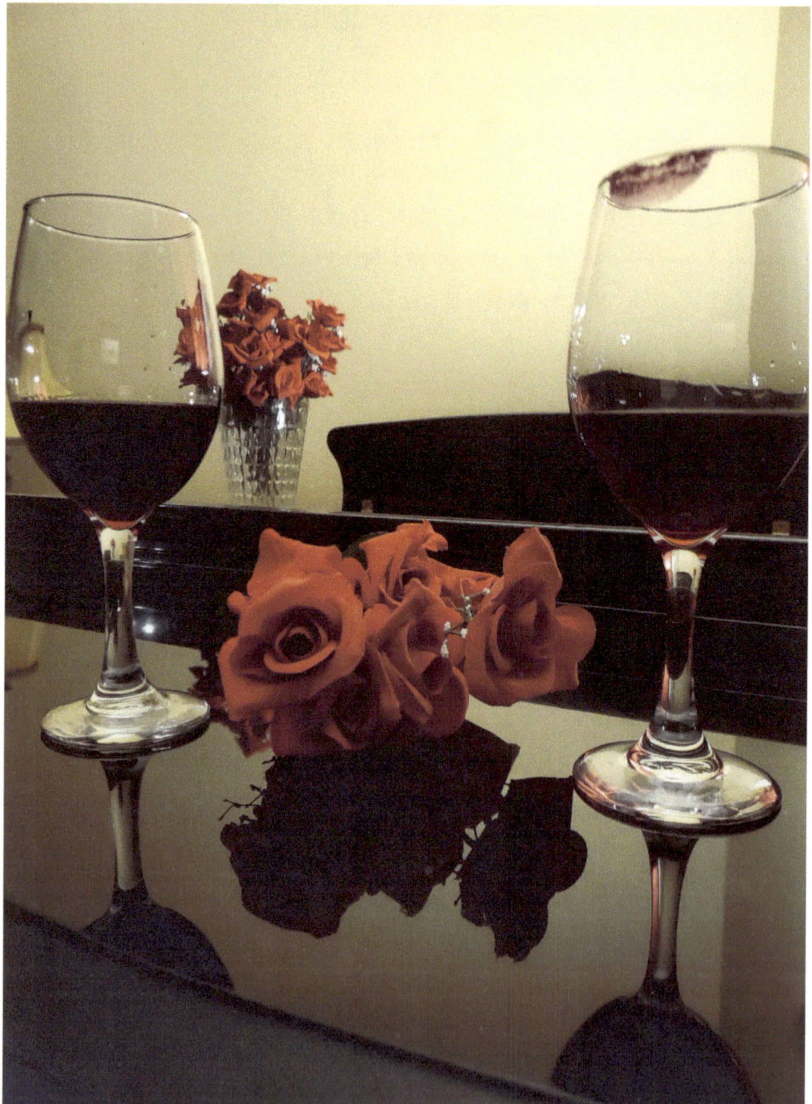

Deep down in my Mind (Lyrics)

When you asked me what was in my mind;
I always thought my mind speaks to me
Now I realize the emptiness inside me
For so long, my thoughts hide within me
Yesterday, when you asked for my thoughts;
Deep down in my mind;
My heart could tell;
Before my body could answer for sure.

It says much of what life has brought us,
taught us, given us, made us
Now, let your heart decide what your mind speaks
Deep down in my mind
I know now what my heart thought about us
It's all about you, for you, and for me...

Why do you wait for my answer to feel me?
Even though your thoughts could read me
Deep down in my mind;
My thoughts stay hidden
For protection, my expressions are forbidden
I don't want to stand alone in an empty space
But always, I've longed for my vacuum to fill with your love
Still you search for more proof from my face
But you know my thoughts could cure
your desire to seek answers.
It says much of what life has brought us,

taught us, given us, made us,
Now, let your heart decide what your mind speaks
Deep down in my mind
I know now what my heart thought about us
It's all about you, for you, and for me...

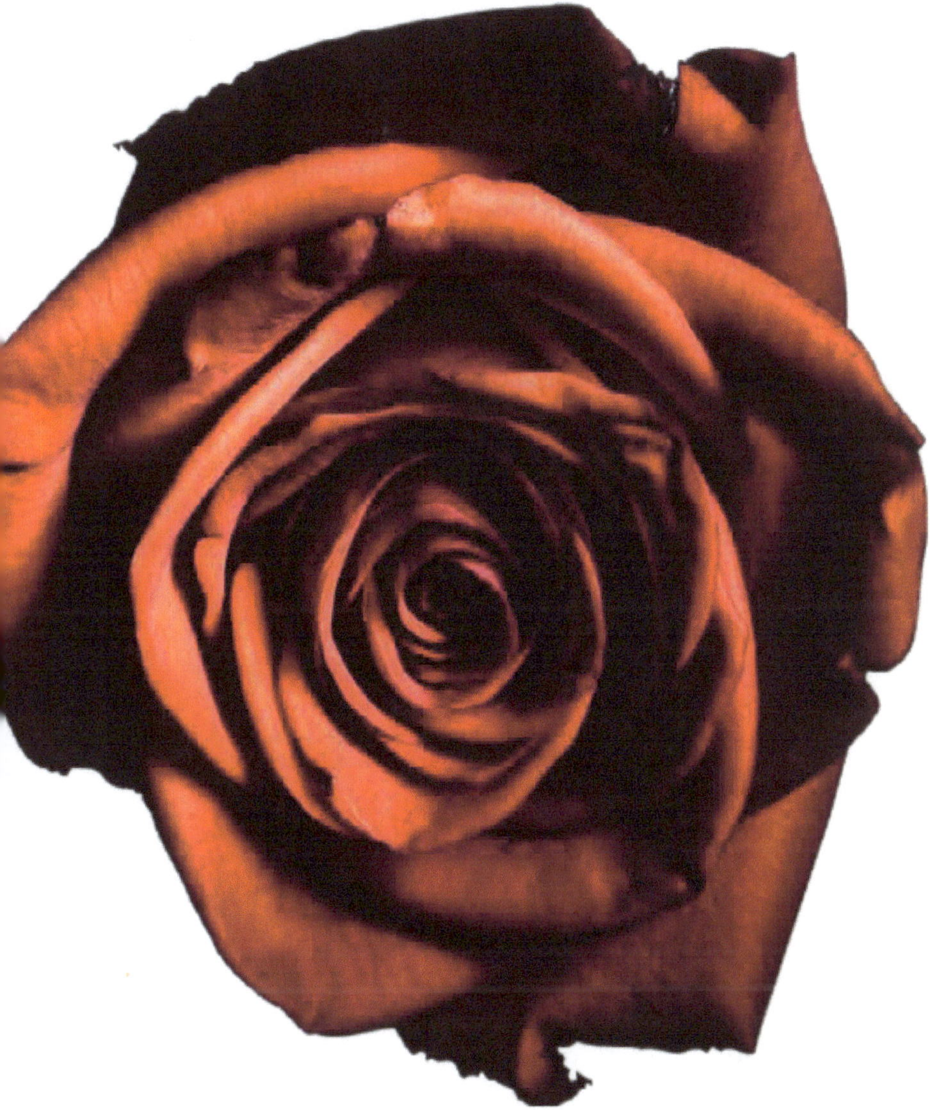

My Butterfly Girl (Lyric)

I remembered she once said;
"I am a butterfly"
In her mind, in her cocoon, she is well laid
She waits in full preparation for her delivery
In her mind, she sees the flowers in the field
In her mind, her wings are wings of many colors of brightness
She yearns for the field of sunflowers and lilies
Maybe a new self with no shyness
My butterfly girl.

In time, my butterfly girl will land on the same soul
In time, the aroma of her decent will reach the same soul
In time, she brings the breath of freshness
At last, my pounding muscles come to terms from her caress
Oh! Yes! She is my butterfly girl.

Now she prances and dances to the tunes of the wind chimes
Her exuberant wings' colors in full display;
So also as she feels inside sometimes
In her mind, she feels the content of her exhale
Now, she is ready out of the cocoon
My butterfly girl is exulted even for the moon
She sees the field of colorful spread as she appears
My butterfly girl is here
She voices her innermost thoughts of smooth caring
As she spreads her lifting soul to feel some loving.

In time, my butterfly girl will land on the same soul
In time, the aroma of her decent will reach the same soul
In time, she brings the breath of freshness
At last, my pounding muscles come to terms from her caress
Oh yes! Yes! She is my butterfly girl.

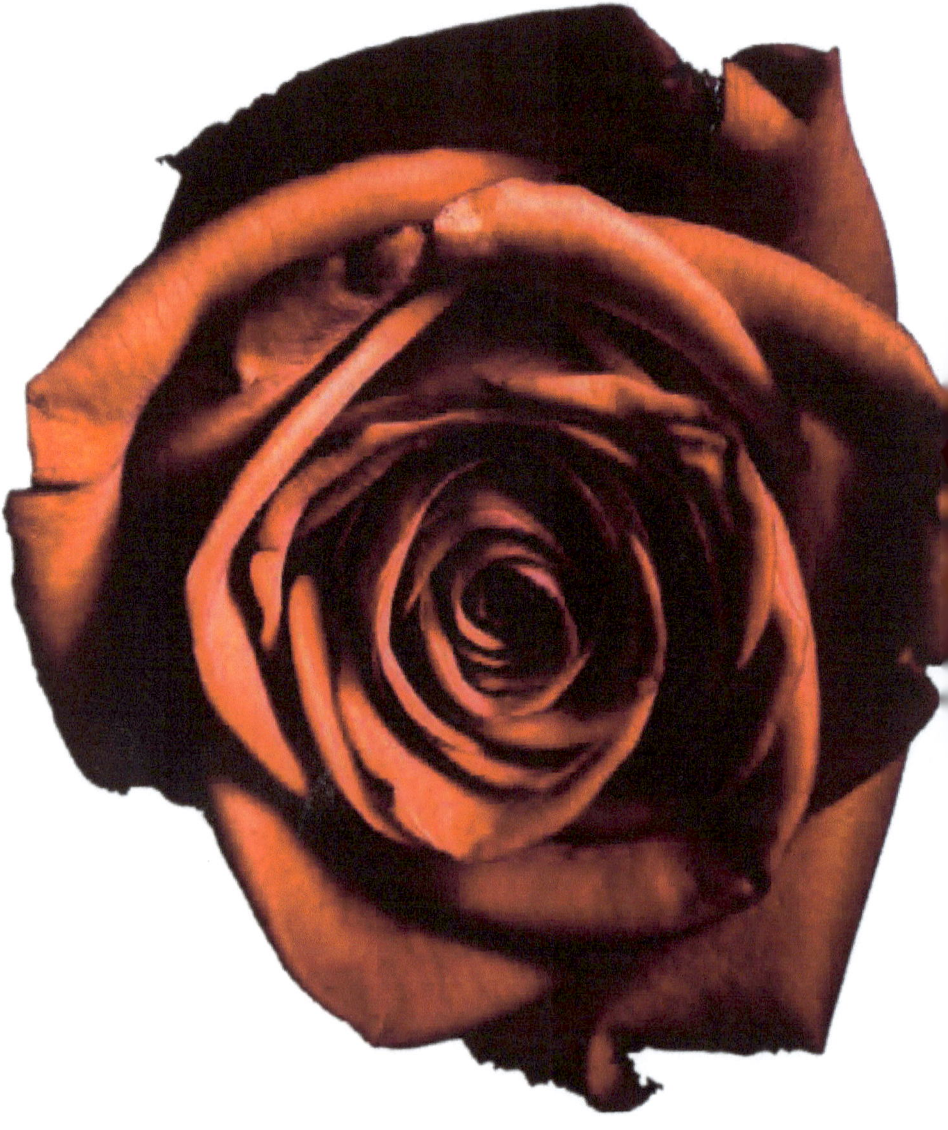

The Light is Out, Baby
(Sensuously Rated)

Face-to-face, we reached at a distance
We ignored the present silent darkness
We read our hearts full of romance
I know your heart; you know what I feel
I feel your anticipation to rock my nature
Yet, my unending desire left me in torture
My goodness! What is happening here?

We reserved each other to borrow love with care
This night, out here, the rain drizzles will soon leave us wet;
Wetness of sweet memories to swim in
The rivers of flowing high-energy stream
You and I; two souls of floating desires
Right now, I see through this cloud
Air moistures dare to challenge, but I stay proud

I can see through any obstruction
I know what I am set to do without destruction
My clean passionate reveal is open to ecstasy
While the dark night clears at the distance so easy
The sound of jazz rhapsody will wake us in the morning
We share the distance like it never existed
So, now the light is out
What's next, Baby?

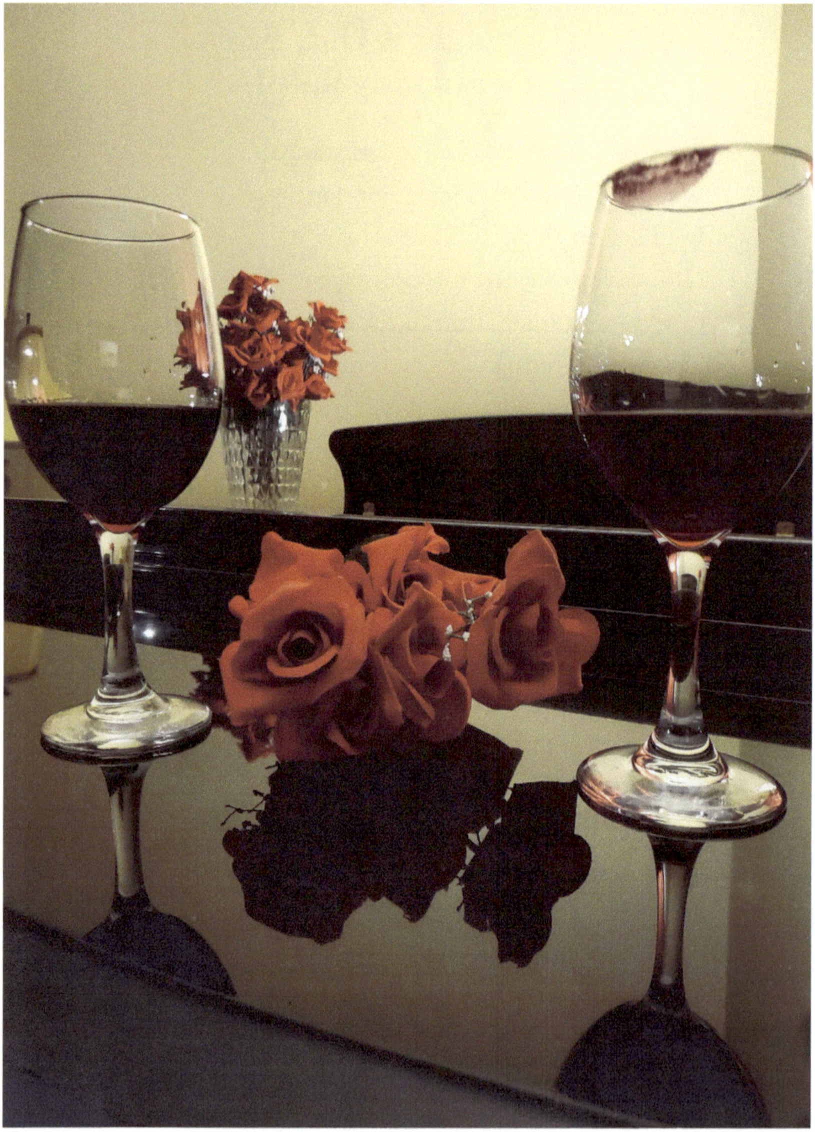

Nothing Beyond Nothing (Ida) (Lyric)

Ida,
She lets air be air
She lets me be me
She lets us be we
She lets herself be fair
She lets her judgment be air
She lets her mind rule her heart
She lets her content float
Here it is, floating like free rose petals of spring

Ida,
She lets her spirit flow in the wind
Here it is, flowing waters of Niagara Falls
How amazing her love travels across the Atlantic
A known destination I welcomed like magic
Here now I am safe, with powers to practice love again
Now, that's an amazing love
The heights never accomplished before and sustain
This is Love.

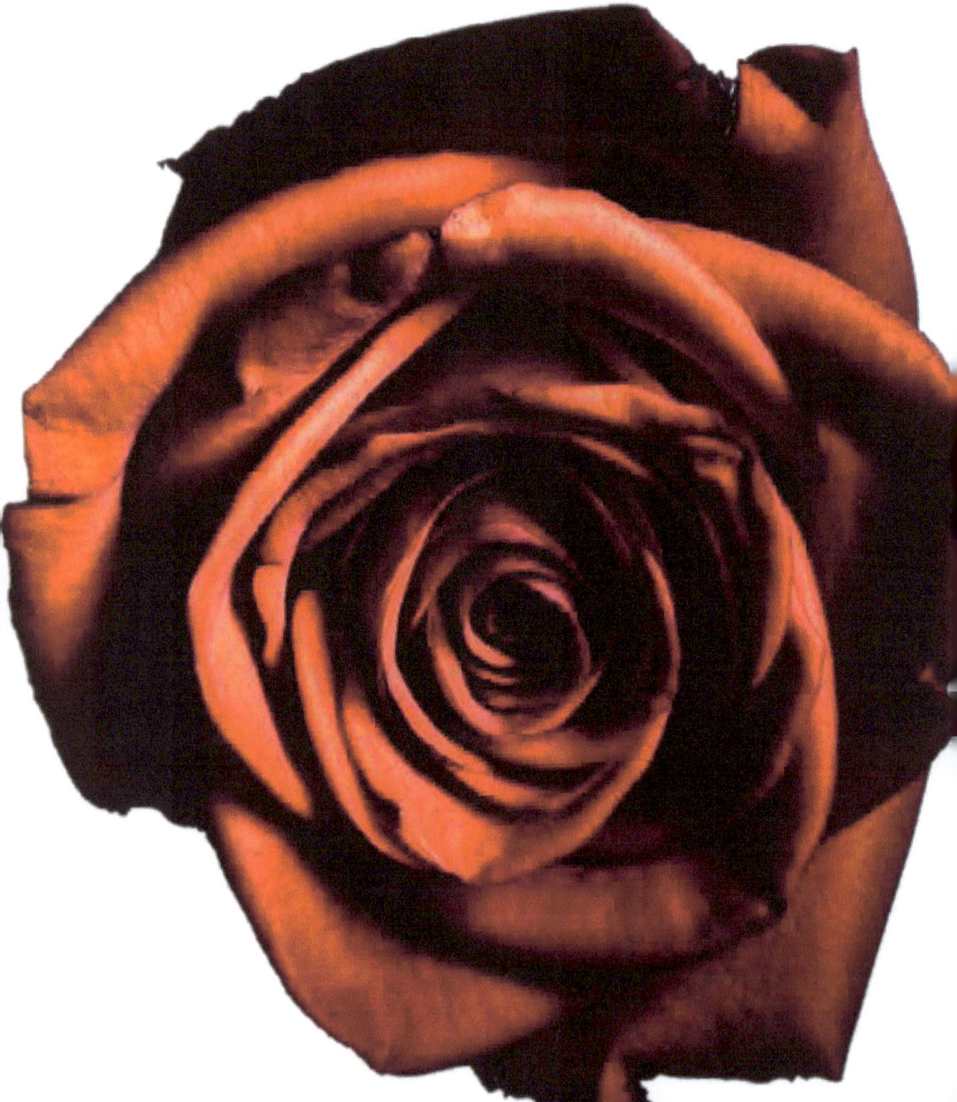

The Village Night Secrets

Yes, I look at you that way
I'm in awe of your love
You spark the sensitive parts of my nature
The stars above could sense the sparkling
While the bedroom holds the secret for sure
Motherland, I am missing you now
You gave me my love for the first time;
To disappear to the unreal world at the drop of a dime

Just yesterday, sitting and admiring a playful stray dog
In the midst of dark evening village nights
My babe whispered to me
It's time another playful dog be mugged;
Mugged by me, as she becomes the victim
Red wine in hand, here comes the muggy me
The room remains silent, as the sunset falls over
We shared our secret, for the night to discover
Soon, morning will introduce the sunlight of life.

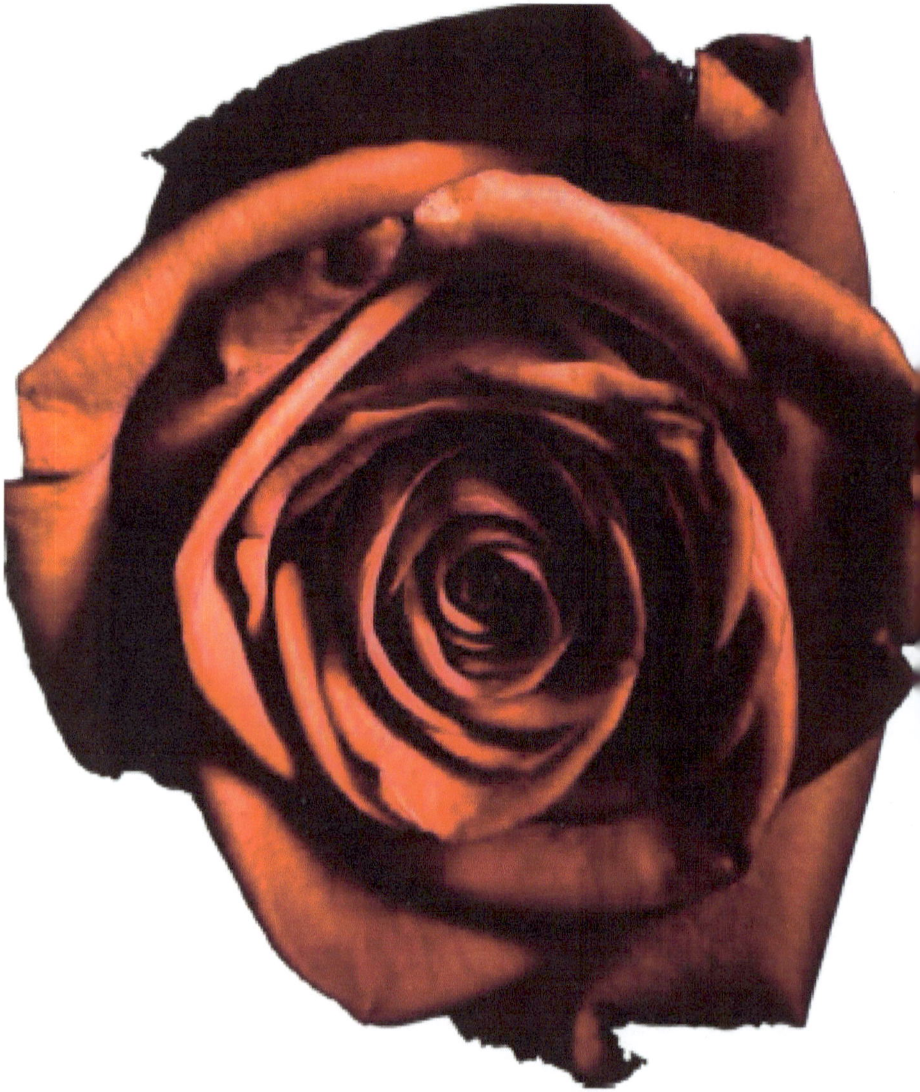

The Way I Love
(Sensuously Rated)

This is me, mi amor
The night came so quickly
The darkness opens the thoughts
The feelings right now sneak in gently
The smooth flow of love you brought
The love stays in my mind
I wrap myself in you
The way I love, nothing is left behind

Deep in the treasures of life so true a feeling
Do I question the nature of this kind?
I answered with everything you gave me
The way I love is kind to me
I respond to your imminent love bonanza spread
See, you are doing it again and again in fairness
Sweetness mellow of desires unafraid

You live yourself bare for sweetness
The way I love, succulent taste of honey
Yes, you did it to me
Your love will never starve me
I am feeding in nostalgic droplets of anticipation
Your love will count my blessings for me

The way I love counts your enticing gorgeous formation
I see you glowing like the sunrise
As you spread your vibes like summer flowers

Tonight, look towards our glorious morning as we dine
Here, the lighting shimmers with the colors of our moment
Wow! Look at your face in angelic glow of colors
It's late night, mi amor
Let's wine and dine.

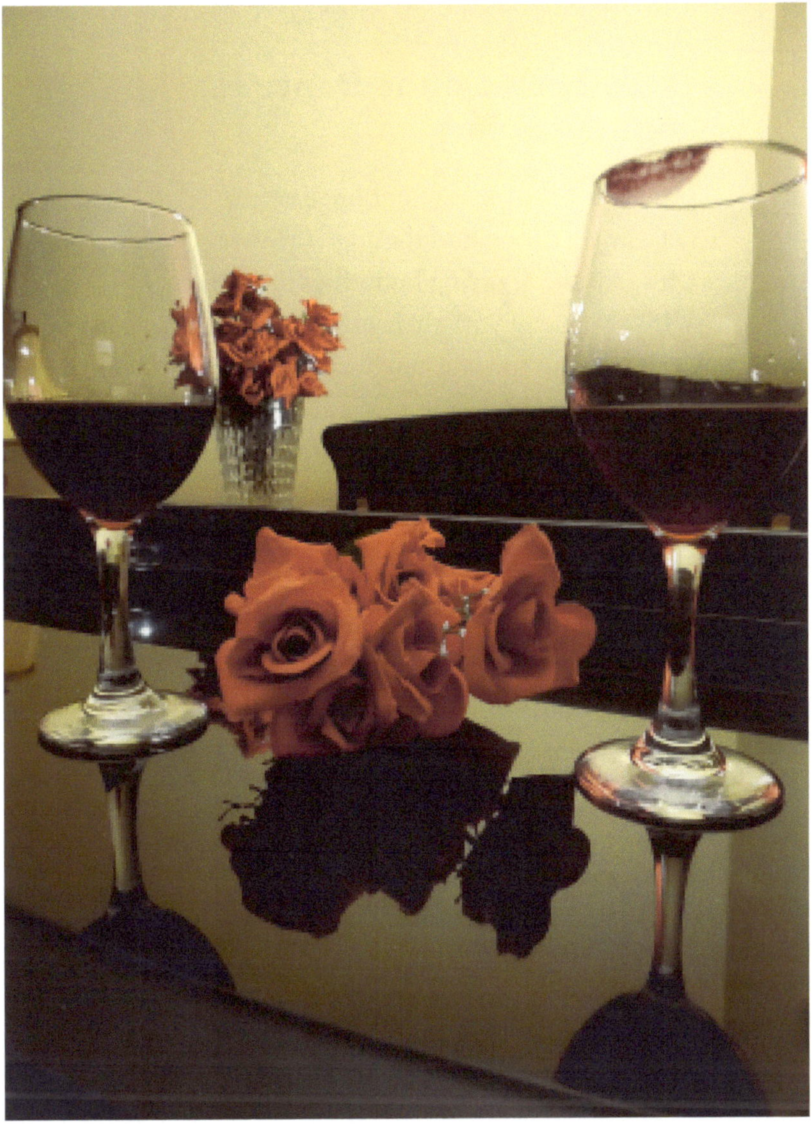

Let's Do the Dance (Lyric)

Let's dance the tunes of our lifted spirits
Let's jingle the bells of the angels with it
Let's join the prancing butterflies in their row
While we blend with their bright colors of the rainbow
Let's dance in the rain and blink with the lightening wonders;
While the sounds of our music silence the roars of the thunder
Let the rhythms of our dancing feet move to the
beats of our hearts;
While our smiling faces see the passion within our souls
Let our eyes meet and greet each other
While our hearts appreciate the joy of laughter.

Let the music bring us together one more time
Let the moment repeat one more time
Let one more time happen some more times.

Let's dance and feel the heat of our sweats
Let's reveal ourselves through our sweaty linen tops
Let's feel the music and keep our bodies wet
Girl, let's do something that we can keep secret
Girl, let's touch something that our eyes can't reveal
Girl, let me taste that;
Ooh! That red Spanish wine, and feel
Oh! Girl, let's get loose and seal the deal;
While these big, red candles fade out with our secret
Girl, let's giggle in darkness;
While we grope to fit our hands with happiness

Oh girl! Let's do the dance in the colors of darkness
Ooh! Yes! Ooh! Yes!

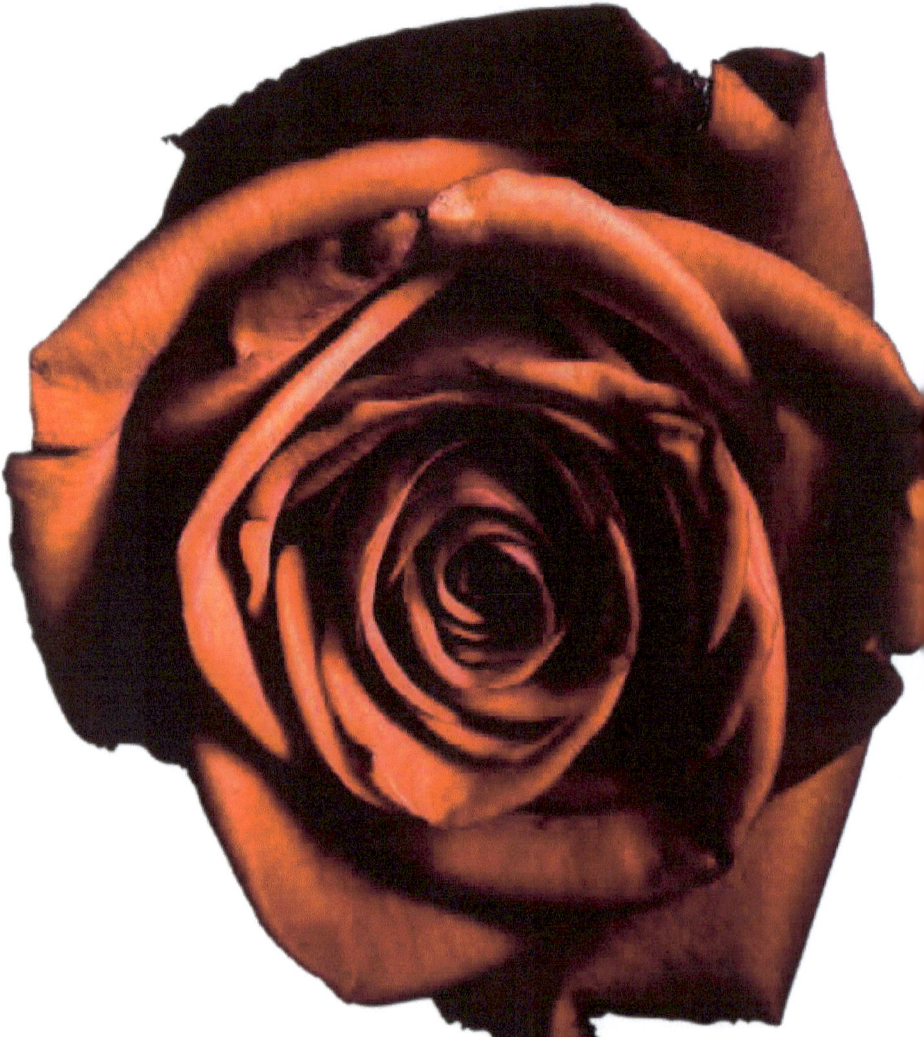

Where are you? (Lyric)

Last night, I started my search;
A search that would lead me to wonder
Where are you? Did I leave you to wander?
In my mind, the question left me to ponder
As I ask myself, "Is this it? Is this it?"

The memories of your last smile
Your last word to me, "I'll be fine"
Here in this small world of mine
I try to answer my own questions
You left my affection stranded in midair,
battered with inflictions
Like a Lone Ranger, I tried to be strong
Sometimes I wonder the state of my turmoil
What could I have done wrong?
In my states of solitude and soliloquy;
I ask; "Is this it? Is this it?"

Your last word kept coming back to me
An uncertain reflection clouds my sweet expectations
But, I'll be here to find you
I'll seize the opportunity
What a sweet anticipation!
I remembered how you told me everything about so much
You are the sole possessor of my heart and soul;
Only to fly away with so much
Still I wonder while I listen to the silence

Out of my deep breath, I could hear the sound of the presence
In my states of solitude and soliloquy;
I ask; "Is this it? Is this it?"

In my dreams, I fly around the dark misty night
Then I search like a hawk to find my prey
Only this time, my search found a glare;
Piercing through the darkness of the night, your eyes
The welcoming dimples of your smile
So once again, in my states of solitude and soliloquy;
I ask; "Is this it? Is this it?"
Then a voice came through the thick, dark clouds
The silence is finally broken, and you my eyes have found
Here you are, wrapped around my flying wings, in my arms
And I hear you say, "I'm right here, my love I'm right here."

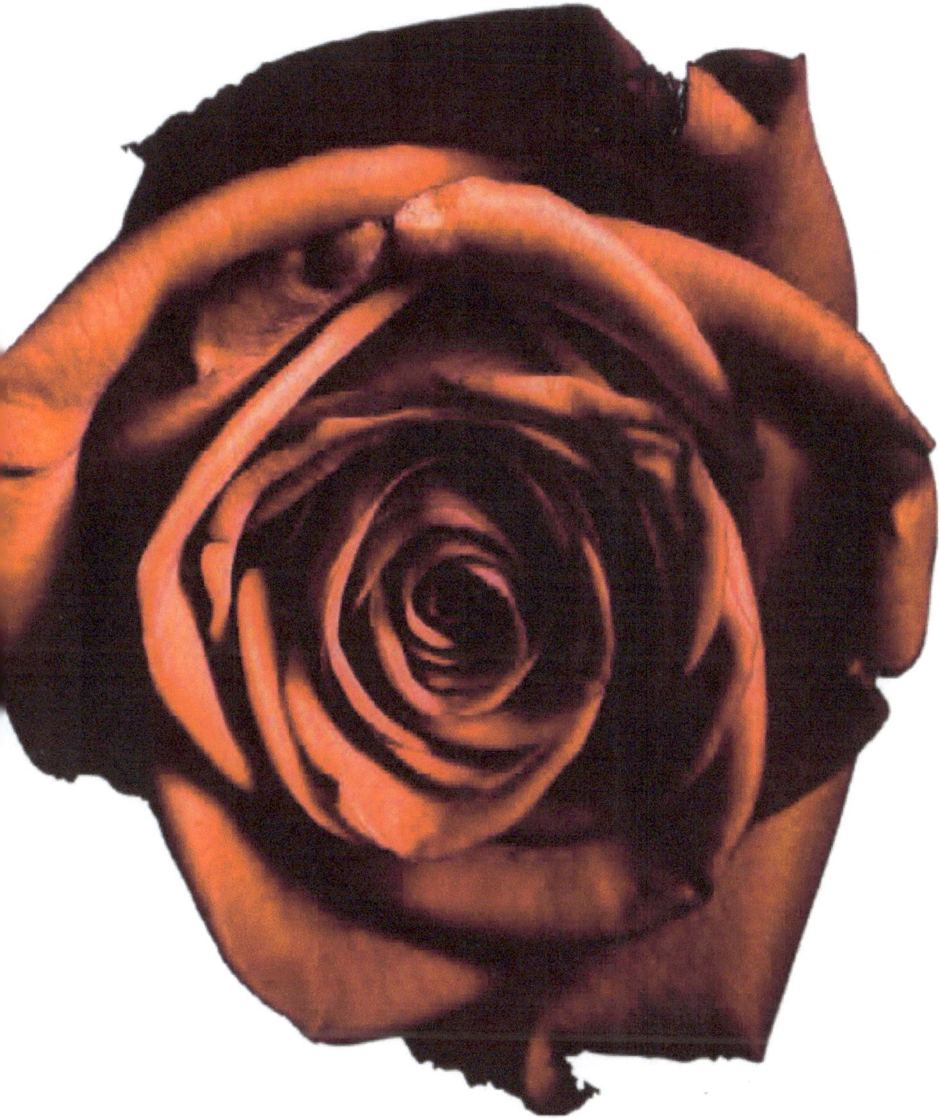

Don't Cry (Lyric)

Why are you crying, babe?
What are you crying about?
The feeling of dejection
The feeling of remediation
The feeling of regret
Why are you crying?
Reach into your soul of existence
The now-remedy is here for love sustenance

Your hands are clean to perfection
The other side remains in imperfection
Resolve a welcoming solution
Are we supposed to cure other minds?
Reclamation of the undeserved is behind
No need of a battered mind under seclusion
Why are you crying?
Here now, you set straight for self-actualization

The lost is a broken emotion
Absence is now a point well understood
Your great individualism is well-footed
Here now, point back to you
Let your stay be amused by your confidence
Let your stay be set ready
Let your stay be you in celebration
Celebrate your solid reformation in relaxation
Please, don't cry.

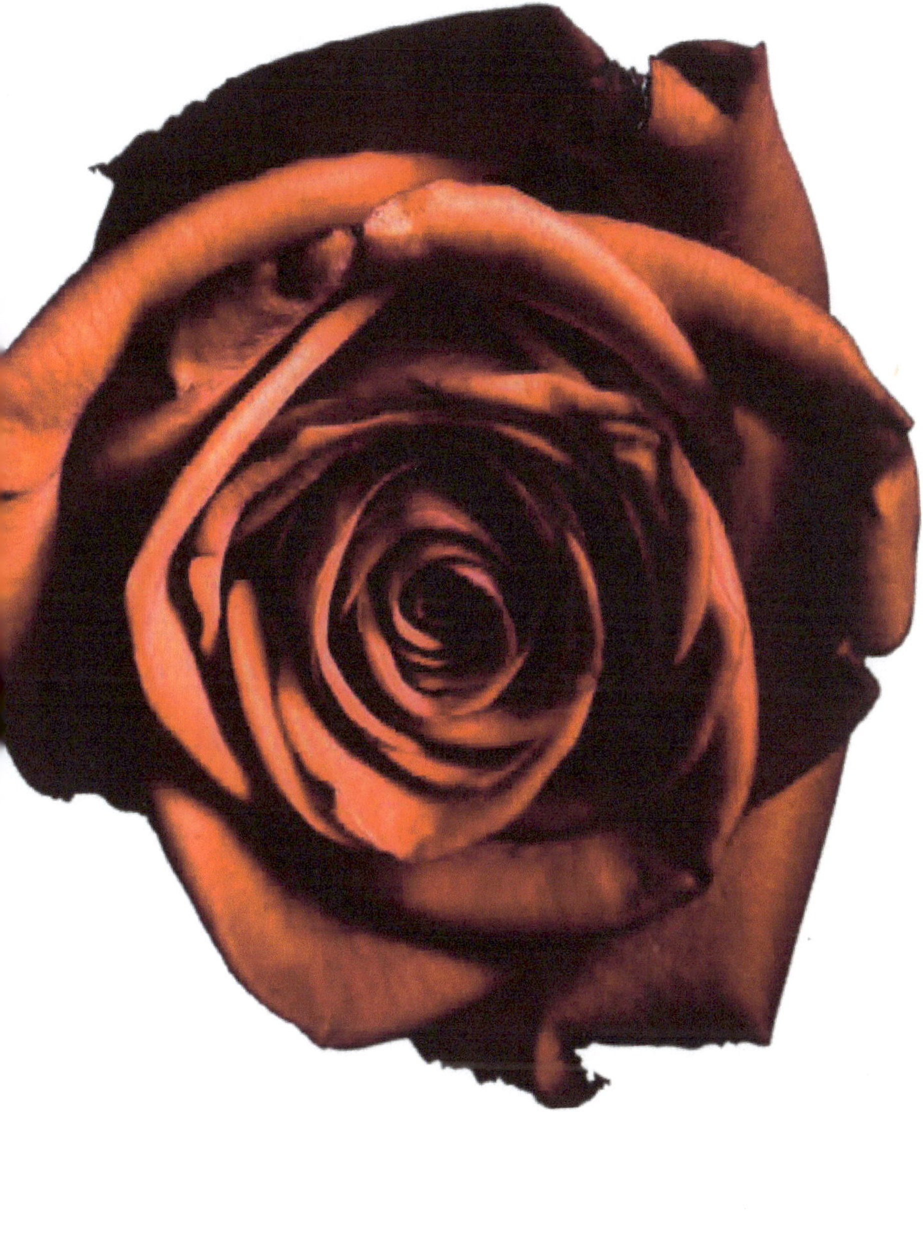

You Missed Me

I know you miss me
Tell me you miss me
Think back to the day that deleted us
The sudden change of spring rising in focus
Give me something for me to reflect
But, you gave me something not to forget.

The trees sway side-to-side
As the wind deflects;
My heart is still broken
I watched your hair float away to elude my eyes
I had thought it might find a resting place in my hands
Suddenly, I'm watching you vanish into thin air
When you called, the air quickly returned my last imagination
Truly, I shiver with anticipation.

You missed me
Now I long for you
Share with me what I missed about you
You missed me;
You are on the rhythm to reclaim our time
The glory of our lost love about to return
Craven a heart resolve so absolute that it will not burn

My heart in a palpitation mode as I answered your call
I did; I answered quickly like I deserve LAUREN BACALL
Again, you have become the new Damsel Beauty for my delight

You miss me the first time
Now, I will not miss this flight
You missed me
Now, let us take this second flight.

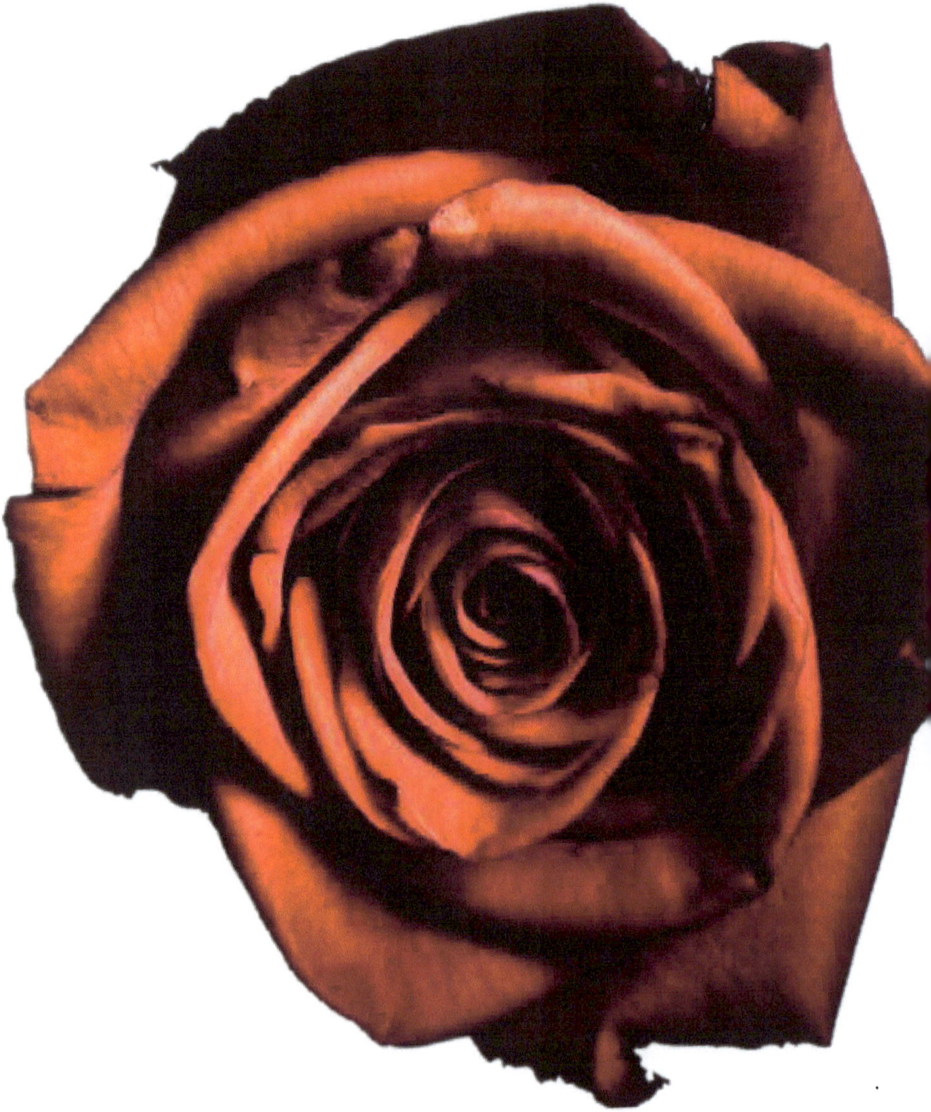

You Fill My Intimate Pleasures
(Sensuously Rated)

Right now, I immerse myself with exhilaration of romance
So true a return to love bargain well induced
Since life offered me a choice of appeal
Now, I accept the appreciation you reveal
Let me escape into the extravagant expectations

Deep down, I struggle to accept love and romance
As we stroll hand-in-hand, here at this pristine lake shore
Cool and calm, the lake waters flow in quiet exuberance;
Reminding me of your consoling sweet whispers
Let me hold you again
Do I deserve this love bargain?
Please, negotiate with me some love to gain

I am slowly falling for you again
You showed me there is no mood spoil
Your blatant passion made me recoil
Sometimes, I am a bit hesitant to resume
Yet, in me, there is enough left to play a tune
Look! The stars are dancing to our tunes
Even the crickets are joining with their melodic chants
I have arrived in a delightful state of intimate amusement
A happy arrival indeed
You fill the intimate pleasures that I need.

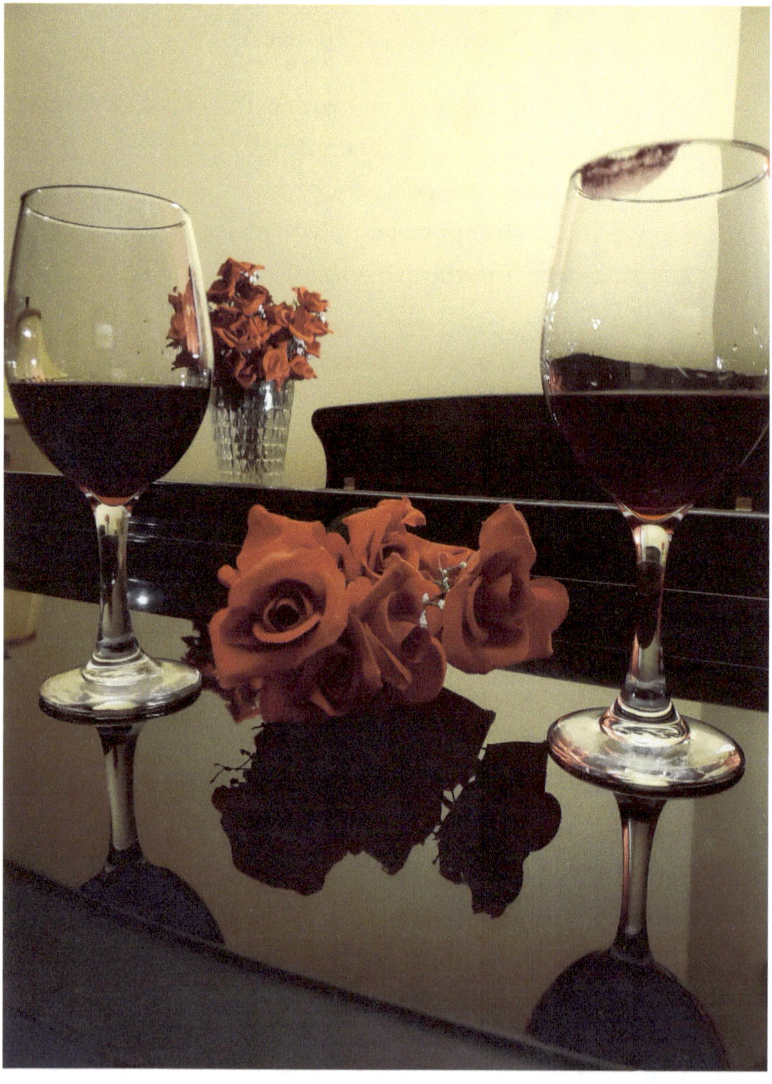

Waiting for her (Lyric)
(Sensuously Rated)

Sitting here, gazing blindly at the screen;
I hear nothing, not a sound from the television
The only sound woke my consciousness;
The chime on my phone
Here she is
I checked my phone
My eyes wide open a reality check

An assuring voice came to my head
Say it, say it; in her heart, she has an open room
'Say you love her;' she awaits the word
Send the word into her deep feminine bloom
She waits, she anticipates as never before
She comes out the shower, wet, and succulent
She waits, she says to me; "Am dripping wet"
I looked into her brown eyes as never before

"Did you hear me?" I asked
Her shower towel slips in rhythm;
She smiled
Warm water drips down her glowing face and skin
Like a stream mingling with tears of joy
"Yes, baby. I heard you," she quietly said to me
Her voice came to me in a soothing sound like melody;
Imagination erupts to wish me welcome

Here she is
I am welcomed into a glorious display of passion
The dripping stream of love potion we shared
I am here; she is there, the bound unbothered
My hands sweats like I am caressing a warm ice cube
She is here with me
I feel her presence in me
I am waiting for her.

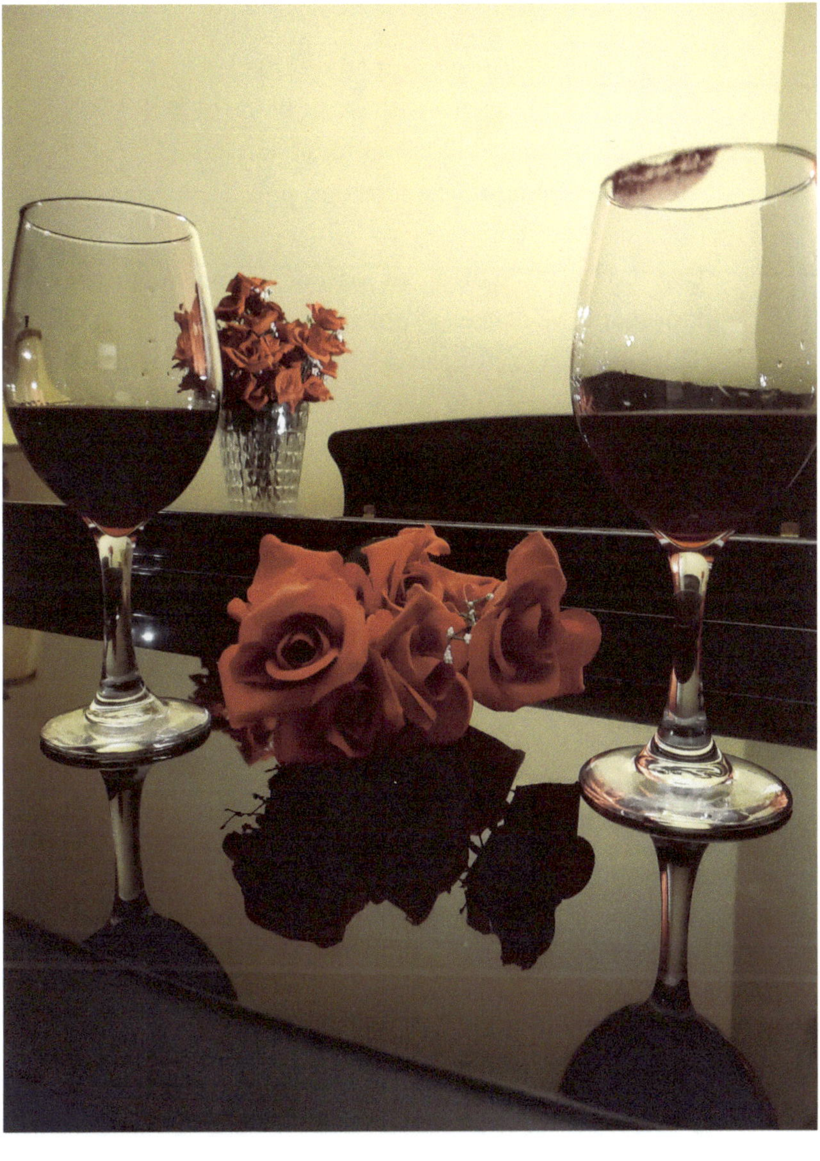

You Loved too Much

You let your heart rule your emotions
You exerted your veins with sweet blood
Like flow of melted red roses for ecstasy mood
The flowers of liquid oil spread to polish someone's heart

Dear Love, let the breakfast toast of the morning wake me
Last night, we danced to our tunes
This morning, we sipped the morning fluid too soon
Amazing recovery like the night still blooms
I love so much to not remember to forget

Did I go too far?
Who called me this time to think about?
Why should I determine the ignorance of romance?
The night was full of baskets of goodies
You tried the cream loaded strawberries, berries, and cherries
Yet, you settled with a sense of reprisal

You love too much for easy reciprocity
You always abated the love promise
Ready, your love refused to compromise
So now, you wonder about a new proposal
Go harbor the deep feelings

Never again you let loose flares of so much love
The feelings leave you to fear
Recovery from a deep love so broken

Did you love too much?
Accept the taste of a miracle love potion to disappear
Drink up and forget love.

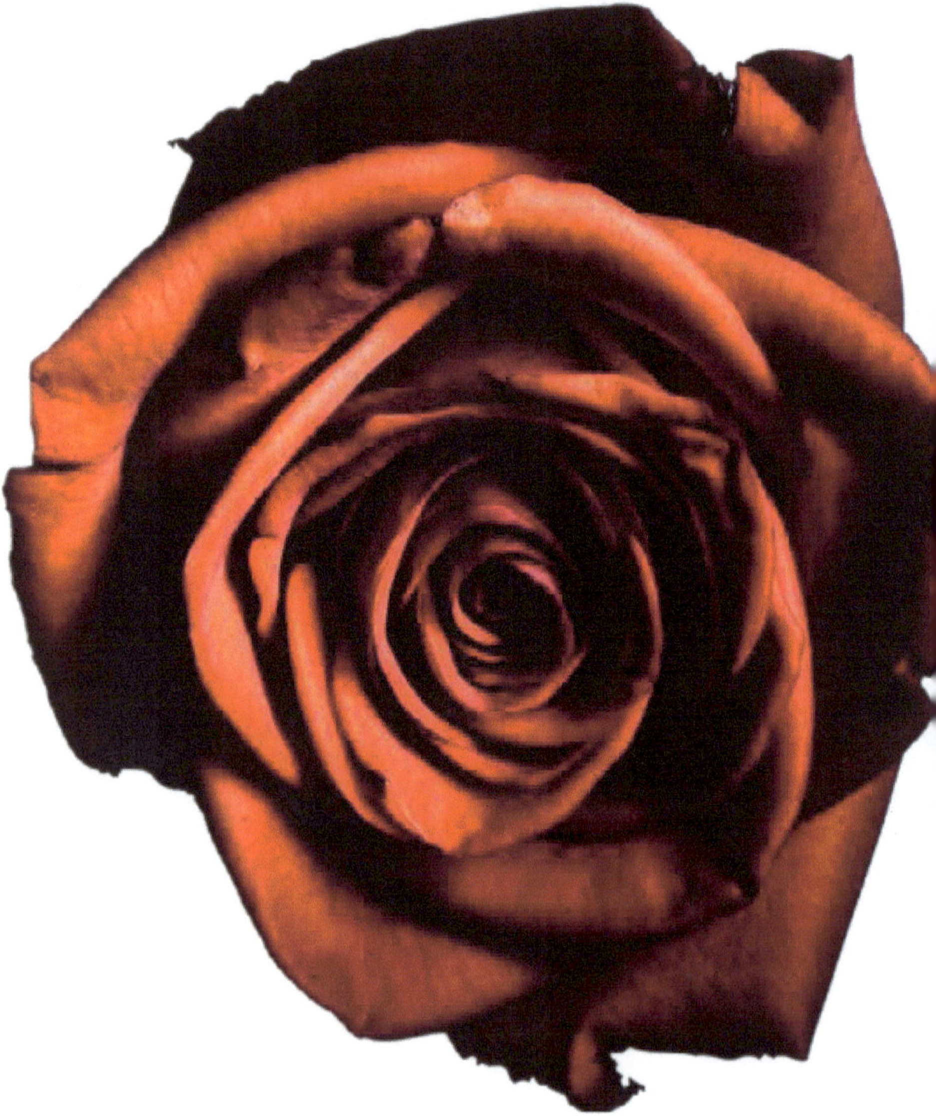

Leave me not alone (Lyric)

I thought I wanted you to leave me alone
Today, my promise never concluded
Still, I doubt my thoughts were never persuaded
I considered the imminent intricate damage
Yet, still to prove my loss of your affection
I try to assure myself I am saving my image
For failures of passion I fail to reciprocate

You still cried to my failed promise
But now, I want you back intact
I left you battered as I vanished without compromise
But now, I remembered I forgot to pack
I tried to prepare for departure
The road ahead felt uncertain for sure

Where am I going without you?
I never meant to leave you not to survive
You said you died from that word to you
I never meant you disappear from my life not to revive
The word came out of uncertain confusion
I never meant to be uncertain of my love;
Your love that I consumed, conserved me with passion

I reserve the passion not wasted in seclusion
I wish you preserved my passion overflow
The real meaning of my story will tell
Like a dream set in the house of cupid

A pointed target that never let go the arrow
I landed and then, I am stuck.

CHORUS:
Babe, leave me not alone
Babe, be with me more alone
Don't leave me alone babe
Babe, be with me to show love perfection done.

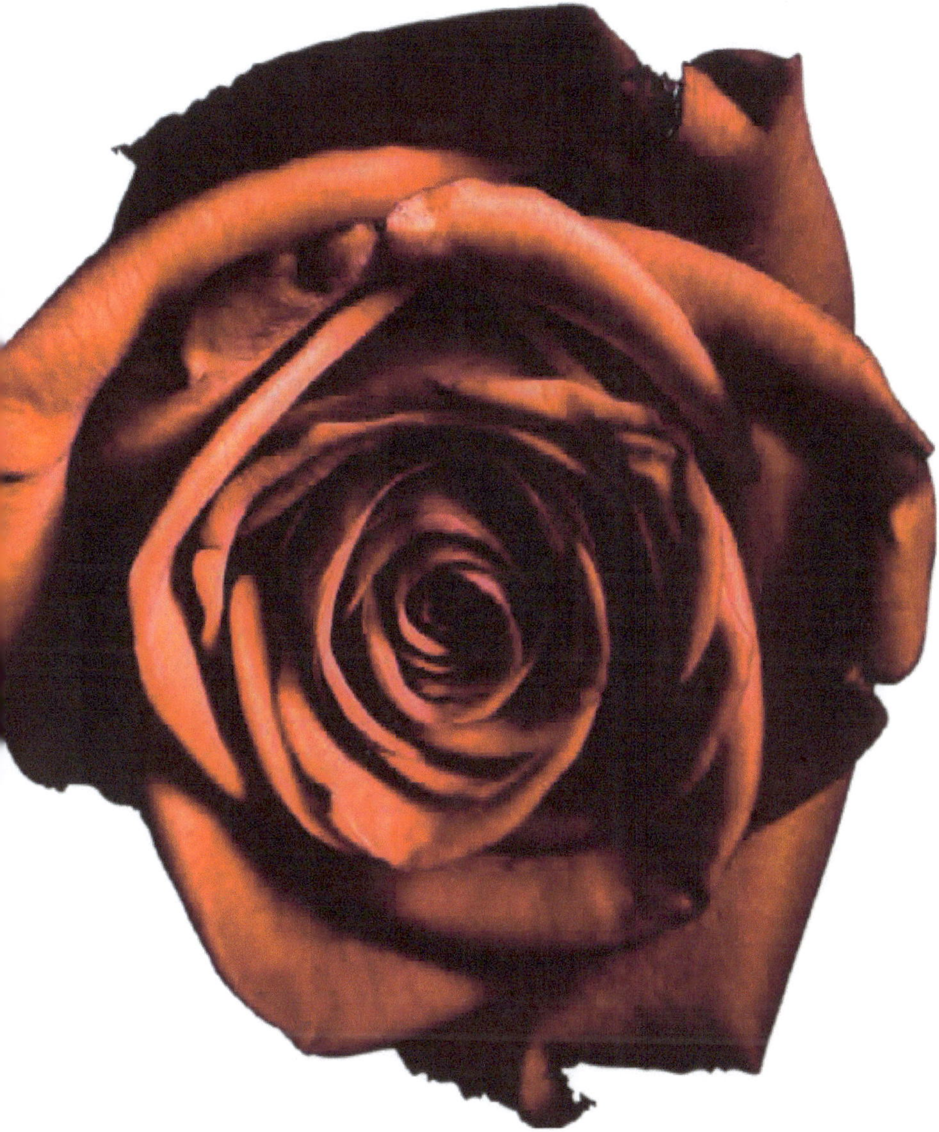

Please Love Again

This room is empty
I am not asking for sympathy
Step-by-step was well defined
Every bit of my love well-refined
No doubt my selfless feelings so exposed
My bare soul vulnerable and uncompensated deposed
My answers so complex and complicated remain confused
Even I have my own questions for my own heart

Like in River Jordan, I expect a renewal baptism
Step-by-step, once again seems to be realism
Oh my goodness! Someone is standing
The necessary exchange we have with Nature
Show hearty love, and then, neutralize the sad feelings
My love holds my deep private resolve
I dread of shivering night chills alone
Yet, love left me a chance for passion expectation
Looks like a bridge crossed and done

The soft knock is here, the door way
wide open without inhibitions
This time is real to feel
My soothing response told the story yet to reveal
I have arrived to play the tune again
Let me play your tune
Let my careful caress recovery gently begin
I will see you for the love sessions soon I will love again

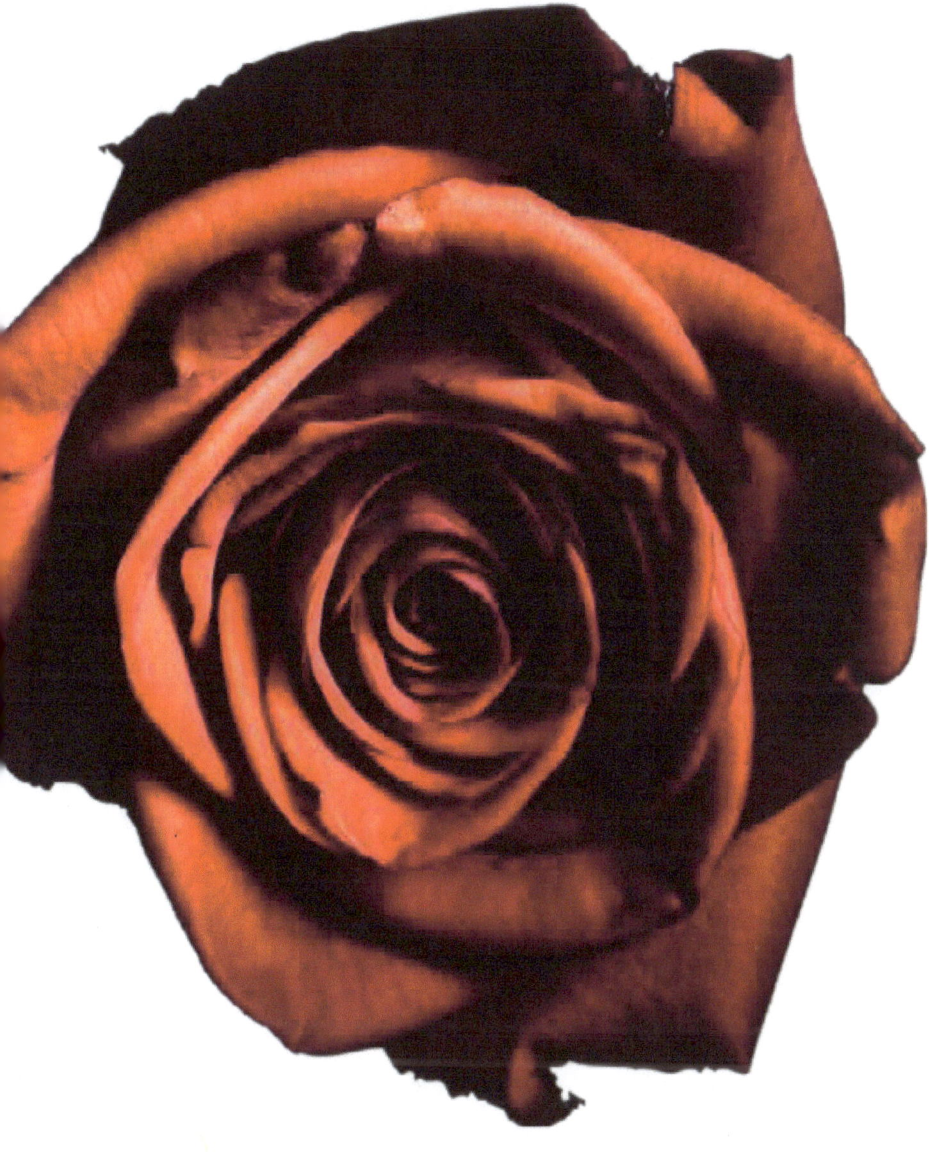

Down the Trail with Bae

Riding down the track on the train in the rain
Rolling around on our backs in the dark
The train cabin coach remained silent to her moan
The music matching the sound on the rail tracks
We were on our way to somewhere, but nowhere all sweetness
Through the window, the world is passing fast in darkness
We ignored the room service to calm passion tension

The cabin coach, small, but suitable for love experiment
Are we there yet?
Yes we are, but not yet for betterment
The rumble and tumble yet to conclude in divine
The train whistles in harmony with her smile
She's a love machine just like the train engine
The comfort we shared on the trail begs for another comfort
A long ride in the cabin coach is what we ordered

The fast-moving train seemed slow to outpace
our intermittent speed
Our natures were responding glowingly in amusement
Are we there yet?
We leave the answer to our love potion
We were love machines in motion
Soon we arrive, but the train was winning the race
We were calm, and then, we actually heard the sound of music;
Leaving our sweaty bodies to conclude the trip
Yes, we are there.

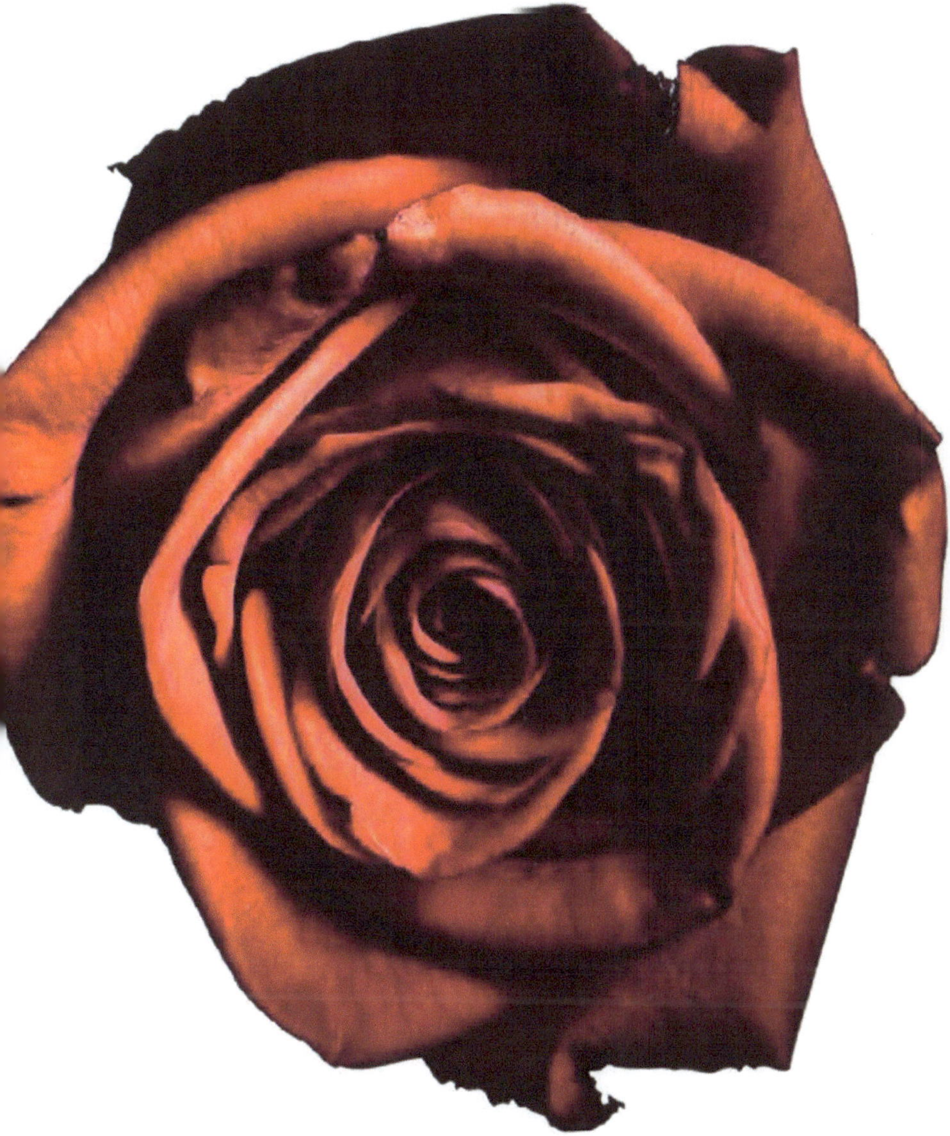

Natural Beauty You (Lyric)

Looking at her short, soft, silky hair;
She reflects the moonlight shine
Her natural fragrance so divine
Her skin polished by an Angel
Her face crafted in heaven
Look at her, see and hear the jingles
from Nature's bell

She smiles in display of self-esteem
Her lips; God-given paint of dark chocolate cream
Her kiss; a taste not to forget
When she speaks; a sound to melt a heart
She sips her aged red wine like the glass
begged for a soft lip polish

Her eyes, a seductive tease of sensuous approval
Her flirtatious wink that arrests a man's ego
Yet, she withdraws from unwanted proposals
Her joviality, a sign of approachability
Yet, her tendencies are uncompromising

She walks in to capture attention that is missing
Yet, she projects a sensibility of comfort
Watch her exude the image of self-actualization
She walks in and directs attention
Her natural beauty receives all the attention
She is really a true beauty of Nature's creation.

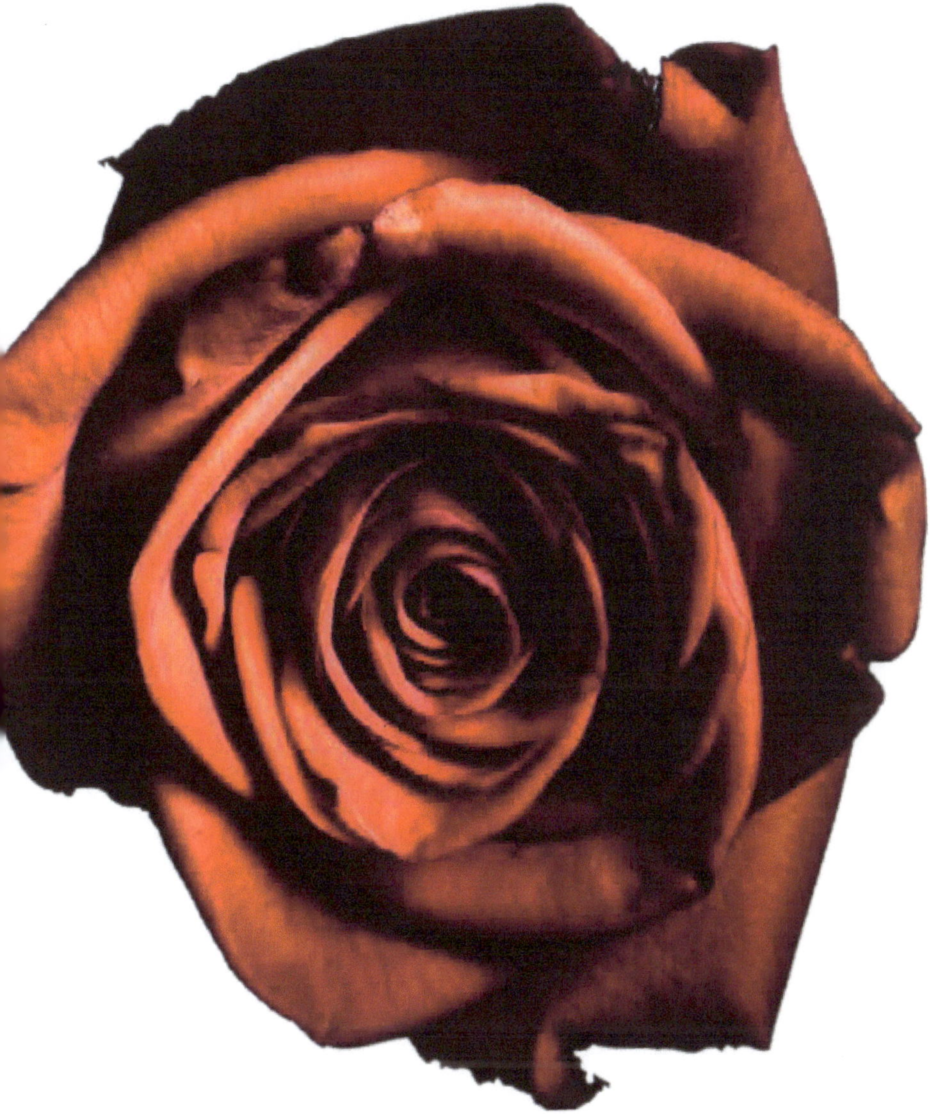

My Life a Music (Lyric)

The strings of violin melt my soul
The overwhelming soothing sound of Oboe
Soaring to the heights unimagined
Your dreams are nearer than you could imagine
Music calls up the senses your brain ignores
The relaxation of mind placed in ecstasy
Here I found happiness like never before
Sitting in solitude, yet filled with a joyful fantasy

Music of life; same music to life
Life never leaves us a note
A music note leaves us life
We release emotions to resolve love
We accept love to pardon emotions
Let me feel the sensation music rhythm serves
Let me feel the passion that I deserve
Now, I rejoice to the Almighty for gratitude

I rejoice to voices that let out sounds of cure
What else will be and could be so pure?
Harmonious voices lightening the earth
Choruses of cheering musical choir in concert
Let the symphony play to echo the evening breeze
Melt my heart with blends of vocal ingredients
The pleasure that reaches the bone marrow to tease
Inside my being, I inhale the sweet melody of saints
To exhale the semblance of unwanted life residue

CHORUS
Give me my music to live
Let me live for my music to reset life
Let the life I live call me mine
Let me call me my music.

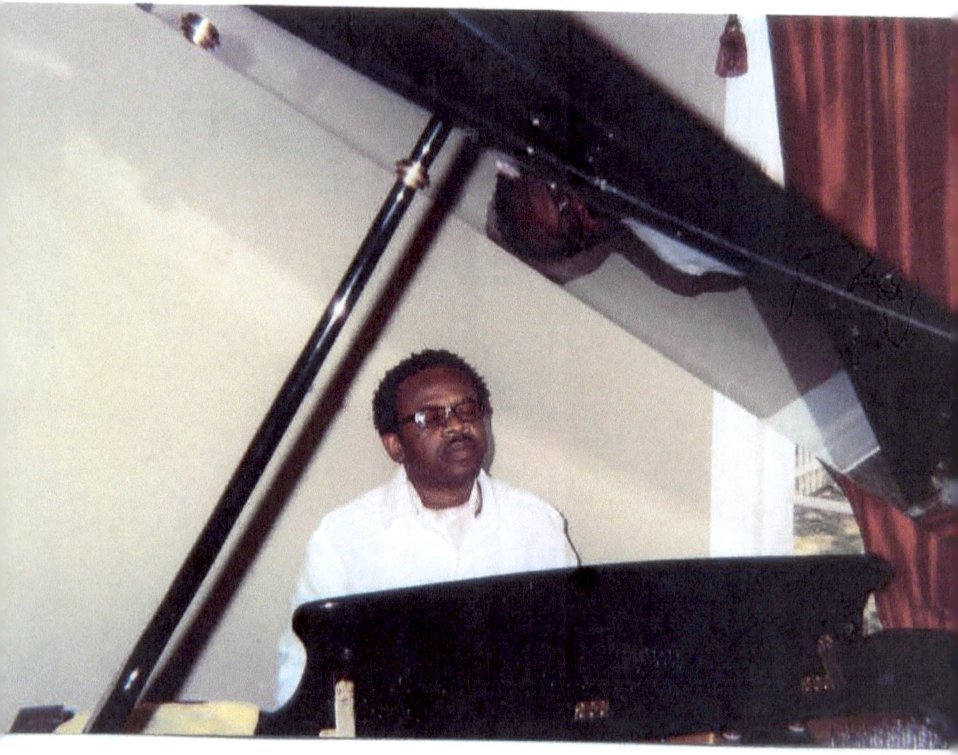

Looking Back

Remembering the beginning evokes the feelings so intense
A true wave of desire reverberate in response
My heart so afraid to let be of yesterday
My reality will never compensate the passion astray
Should I look back?

To dismiss the psychic melancholy of wanting to stay
What will be left behind of my world in torment?
Determined not to invoke the spirit that is crying in self-pity
Yesterday reveals the flawless passion that left no comment
So deep into my soul that I searched for liberty
Should I look back?

Sometimes the heart's passionate response remains inevitable
What can be said of a broken heart must stay extinct
Excuse me while I tear-up for a love story that is distinct
Here is the trilogy of soul, heart, and mind inextinguishable
Still the remaining story does not match the expected end
Should I look back?

Why should I dwell on the whole notion of self-defeatism?
The power to retreat must hold under strong anchors
Let the mind lament to the departures never restored
While I retain the good part in cherish
Everything about lustful memories is almost childish
In the end, still, I refuse temptations to look back.

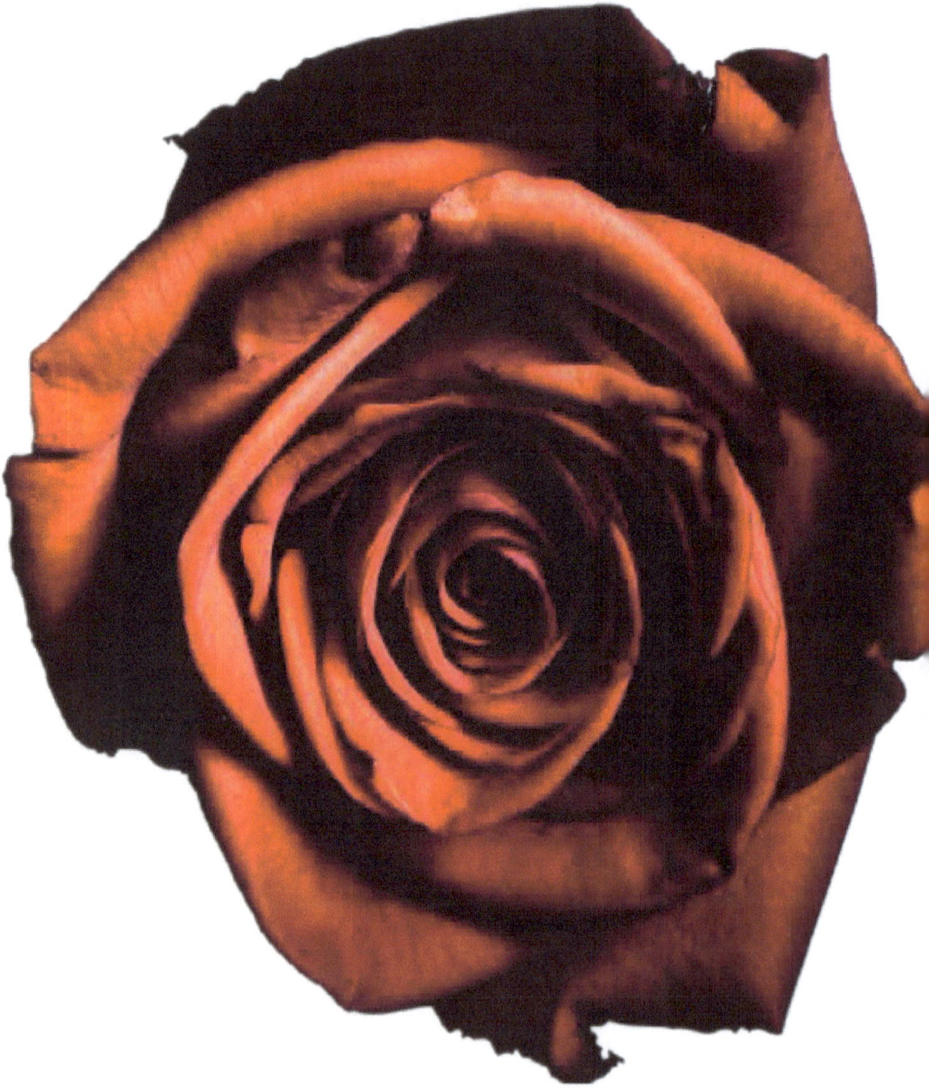

Reserve your Strength for the Day
(Lyric)

Solitude, solitude, solitude…
The night, the glittering stars
The moon communicates to the glittering stars
Letting the stars shine for a brief moment
As the moon overshadows and becomes the light
As intended to give the world its brightness
As intended, spreading the message across the universe

The stars come across at a brief momentous brightness
The stars relent, while the moon spreads the brightness
As we see it as the full moon the darkness hides
We still listen to the night owl singing across the darkness
The moon suddenly exposes the darkness light of the world
The settlement of the abandoned Nature in secret

Yet, Nature will come alive in the morning
Giving us the sun and the day
As we celebrate this day
We give thanks once again to the Almighty
As we reserve the rest of our strengths
Now, we must reserve these strengths for the day
We reserve our strengths for the rest of the day.

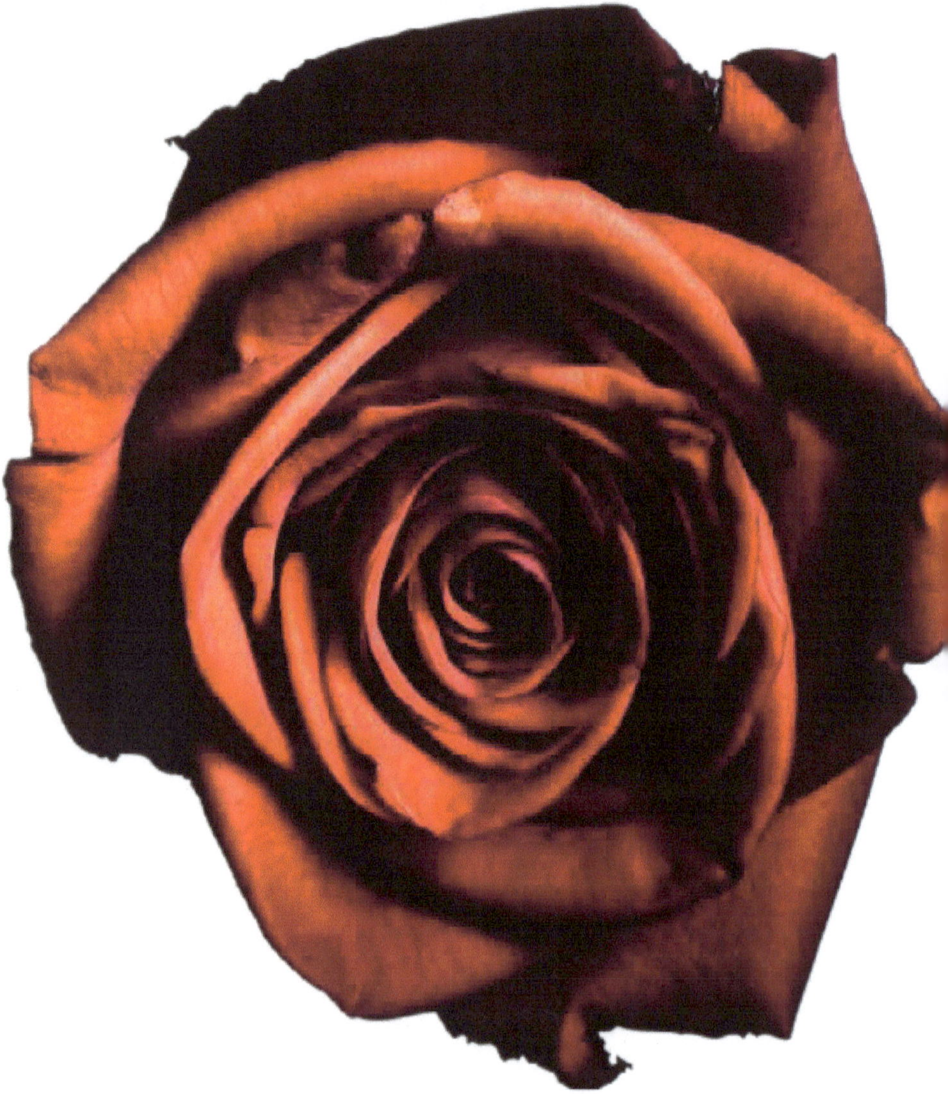

The Things you Admire (Lyric)

Listen, the quiet, the solemn, and the sound;
Coming out of your fingertips
When your mind overshadows events around
And your fingers speak
Leave all the worries around you
Let your mind rule your soul for you
Leave all your worries around you
Let your mind speak through your fingertips

Your dream manifests into your soul for you
Let there be no doubt, your heart rules in beats
Your mind and your soul control your emotions
The emotions devoted to your entire life on the beat
Your life is the essence of your living
While your spirit controls everything
Leaving your love for the things you admire
The things you admire
The things you admire.

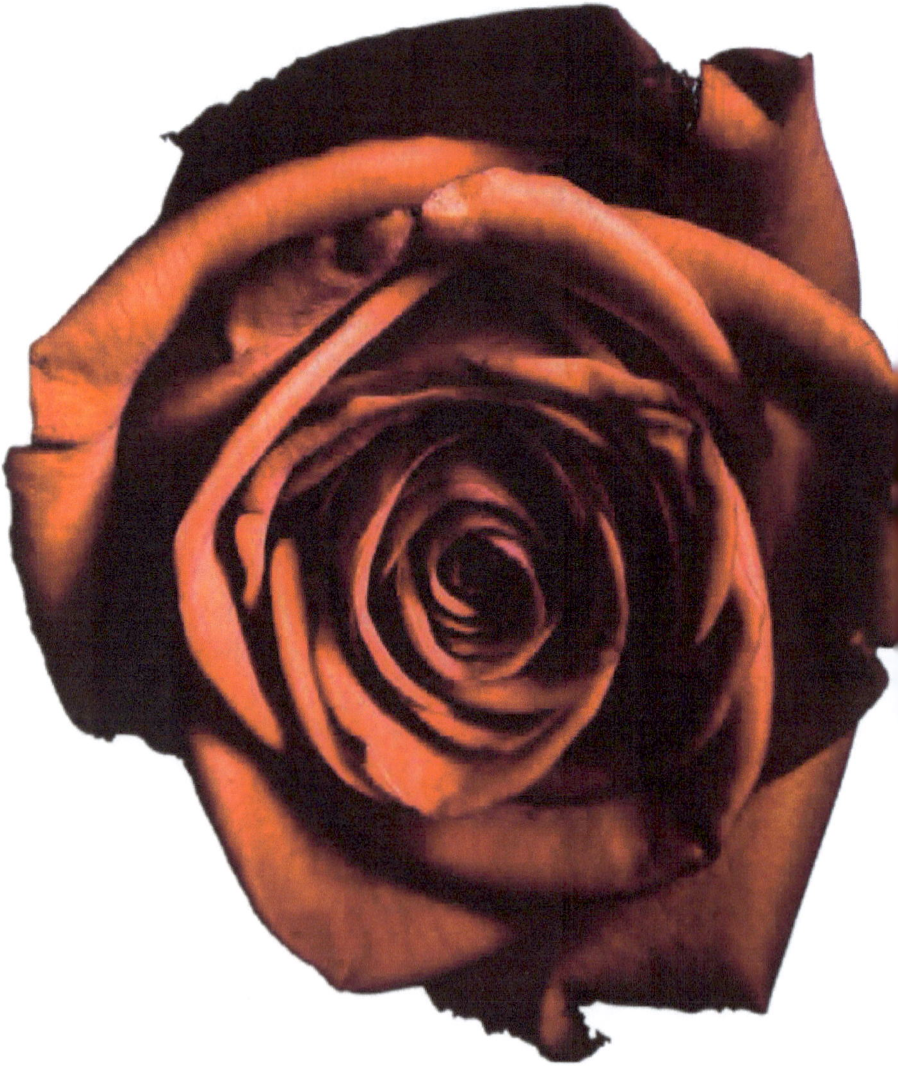

Let the Flamingos Fly (Lyric)

While you look for me;
I left for the long journey
I took your heart
I know it belongs to me
It took all the strength in me to leave
For I know the road will stay open
The road comes bumpy
Not enough for my dreams to dampen
Though I know it doesn't come easy

I will shine like the summer flowers
I will walk to the flamingo's rhythm
I will dance to the sounds of the summer birds
I will sing to the rhythm of the rhapsody chimes

When you ask me how far
I know only one mind can determine
When you ask me how sooner
Soon the streetlights will shine
My tears will not be in vain
Sleepless nights will bring sweet fulfillment my way
I will shine once again
For I know that your heart is in my soul to stay
Ready to do the flamingo dance with me?

I will shine like the summer flowers
I will walk to the flamingo's rhythm

I will dance to the sounds of the summer birds
I will sing to the rhythm of the rhapsody chimes

Here and now, I am in the lights
The colors so bright and wonderful
I look at you to see your strength
Your soul so uplifting is beautiful
Your smile so radiant even to the stars

Now, heaven opens to accept my hands
While the stars shine for brightness
I know it is my turn for happiness
I will be shinning with the stars.

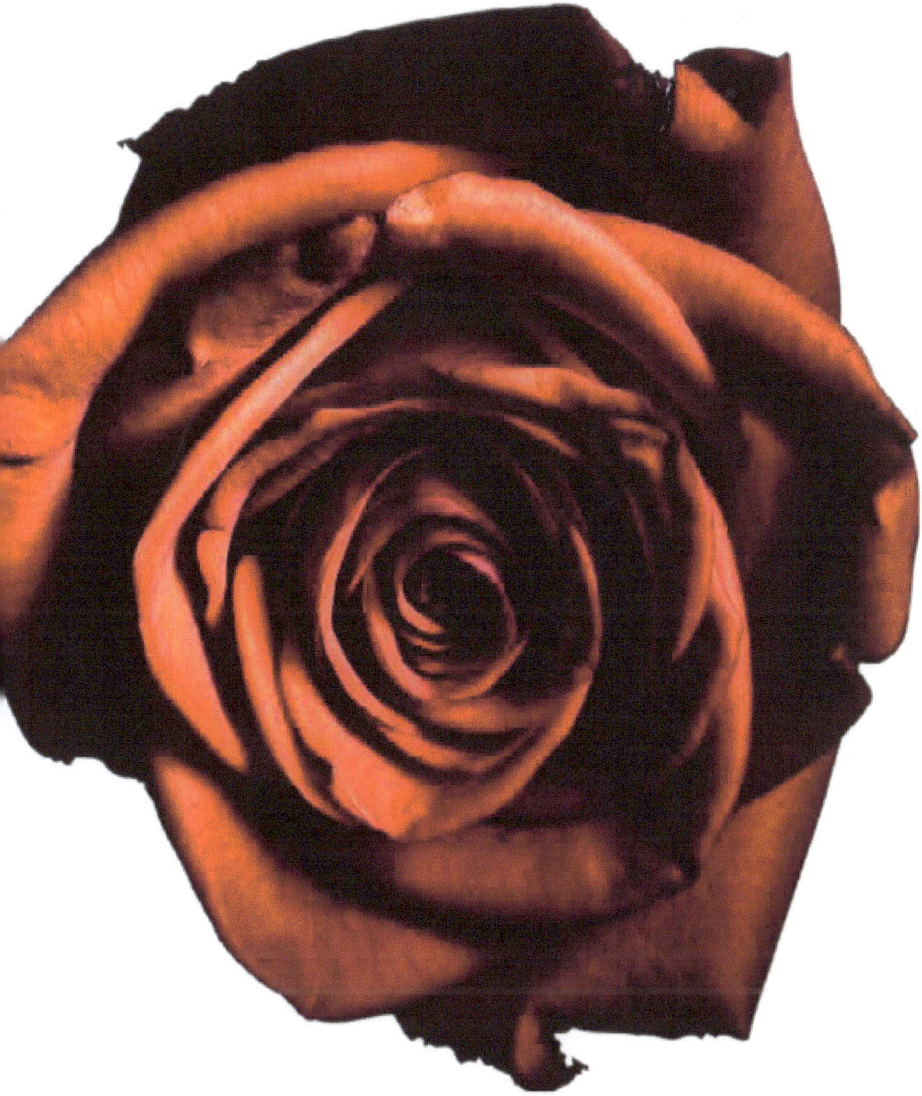

The Mind of Orlando (Lyric)

Come inside the heartland of discoveries
Where the hearts of children are full of joy
Their smiles, high energies of life's fulfillments
The heart of Orlando
The great sites of wetland amazements
Welcome to my Orlando
Your fantasy heaven is the mind of Orlando

You made me make up my mind
It is the mind of Orlando

Come inside the spirit of Orlando
We capture your desires to please your children
The dreamland of Disney
Where Mickey's friends say hello
Where the minds of our children match their fantasies
Welcome to my Orlando
Your children's delight is the mind of Orlando
You made me make up my mind
It is the mind of Orlando.

See faces of the children of the world
The daily bread of our souls seem to reveal
The love for our children here stay unfold
Here, happiness of family is rooted for real
Then, we say welcome to my Orlando
Our cheers of joy receive your smiling faces

And this we call the mind of Orlando

You made me make up my mind
It is the mind of Orlando.

Come see your anticipations match your expectations
Here you fulfill your childhood imaginations
The clean air of Seaworld; the magical landscape of Disney
Calls for a Hollywood Studio inscriptions
We see the universe like it is in the movies
Now, we made a safe heaven here
This we call the mind of Orlando.

You made me make up my mind
It is the mind of Orlando.

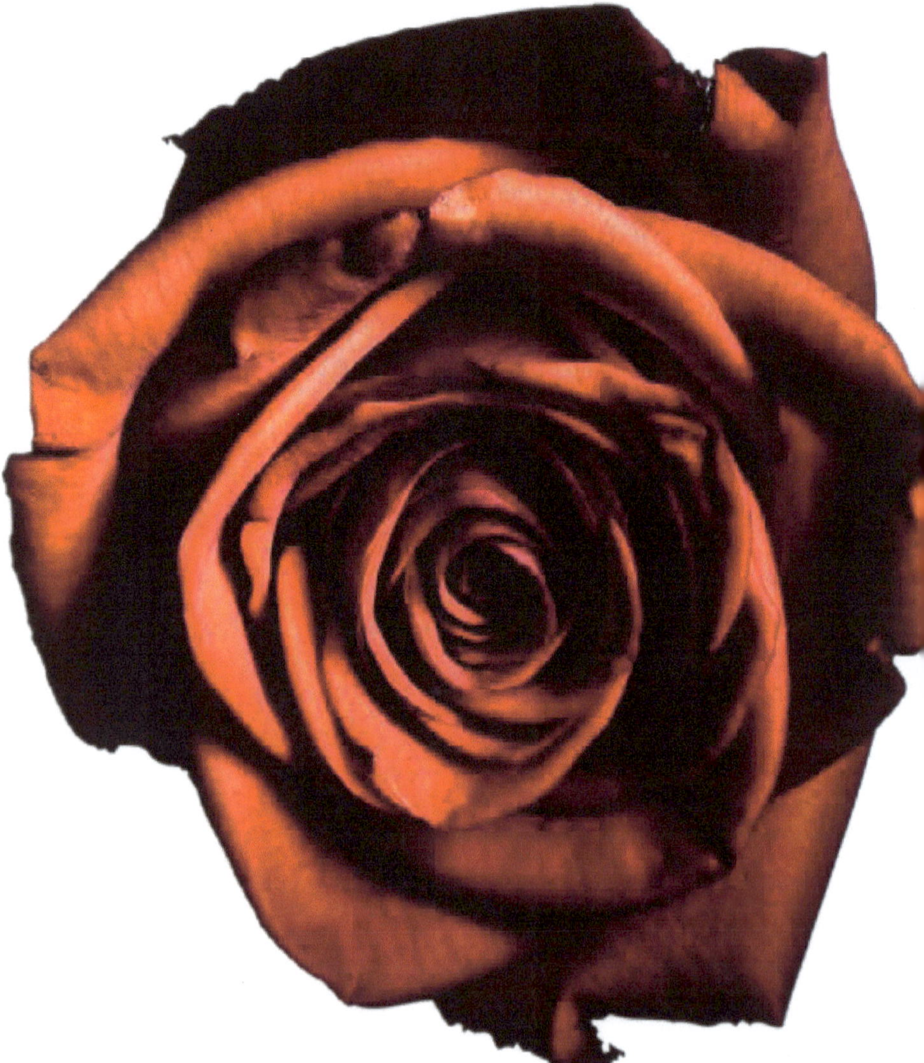

I don't see color (Lyric)

When you're sitting in the bar in a party mood
The bartender filling you up with refills
You tap your feet to the beat of the music that you feel
The bartender pulls the tap to make someone happy

So, look around you and move your body
The flashing colors of the neon lights are the colors you see
So, look around you and move your body
The colors of the flashing neon lights bring us together
So, look around you and move your body
The mood in the club is for everyone to gather
So, look around you and move your body
Let us see in each other's eyes the fun of partying together
So my friends, join in and enjoy the beat forever

The neon light is the only color I see in here
Don't waste your time thinking about who is who in sight
This moment brings everybody closer in here
Don't ruin your chances of good times and fun play tonight

So, come on and dance around the flashing colors of the lights
When you don't see color, you get the play
everywhere and more
So, look around you and move your body
When you don't see color... ohm!
Ohm! Ohm! You're wide open for more
So, look around you and move your body

*When you don't think about color ... ohm!
Ohm! Ohm! Loving from all angles
So, look around you and move your body
When you don't see color, the music moves
you closer to mingle
So my friends, dance to the beat of the music
Join in and enjoy the beat forever!
Forever! Forever!*

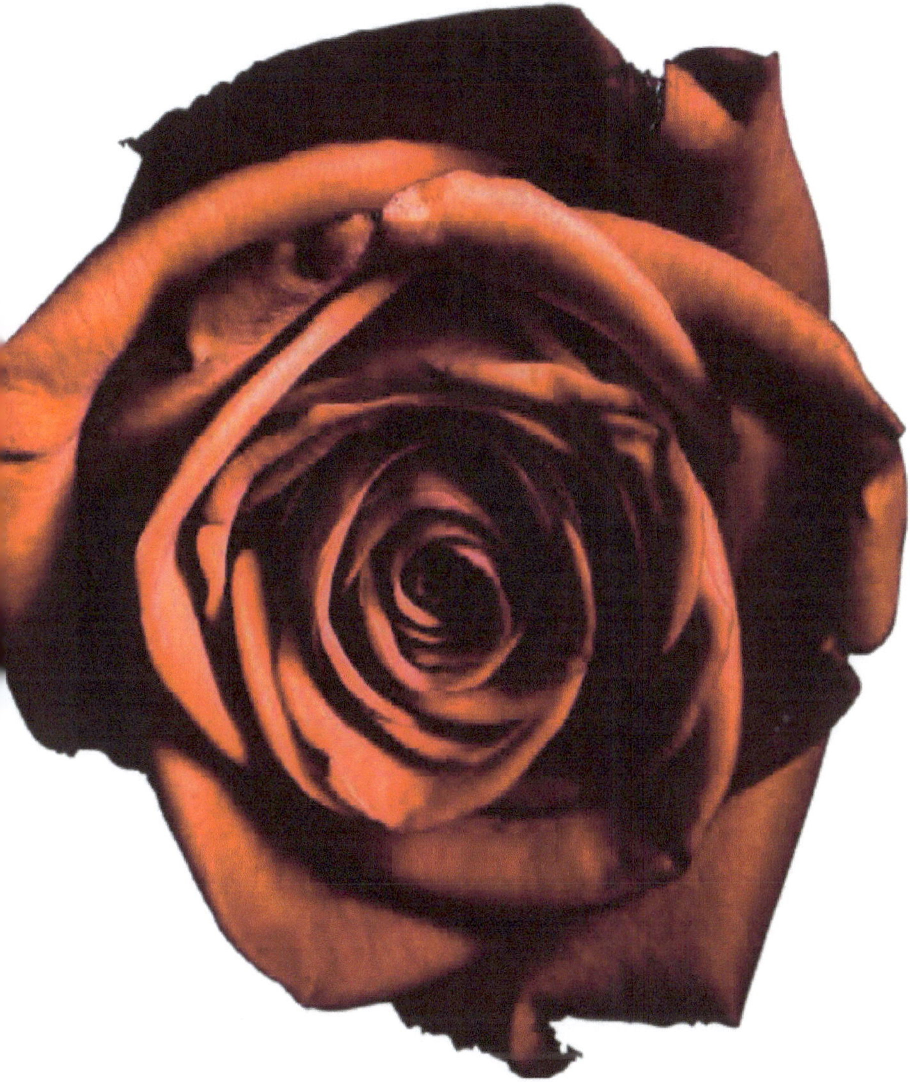

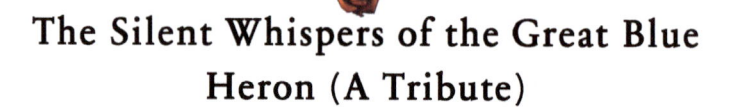

The Silent Whispers of the Great Blue Heron (A Tribute)

The sunset begins
Its fatigue and weakness all over again
My intermittent yawns stay dry
Like crocodile waits
Mouth wide open with no gains
My weary yawns stay dry
Intermittently it comes
But no gains at rest
Mother is still ill
But her hopes I feel
I will stay with Mother
In spite of my fatigue

My feelings stay weak at dawns
To my face depression boasts
Suddenly, the chipping birds tell me it's dawn
My unclosed eyes open to see the morning dew come to pass
I can smell the morning freshness outside the windows
Yet again, Mother cannot feel even a shadow
I will stay with my Mother
If only she can see the Nature of dawn now
Out on the shimmering glaze of the bay waters
Textured by the blessings of the morning sun-drops
The flowing water looks cool and calm
Oh! Yes! There she is!
Cool and calm as she stands

Her color matched to her natural surroundings
She stands cool with intent
Patiently, she awaits the next meal for content
The meal the water will bring
The Great Blue Heron
How patient her life can be for being
Out of my eyes they are falling
The tears of my yawns
While I remember this dawn
Today, I leave Mother's site
But the Great Blue Heron, though silent at my distant site
My gift she delivers this morning
Her silent song my Mother will hear.

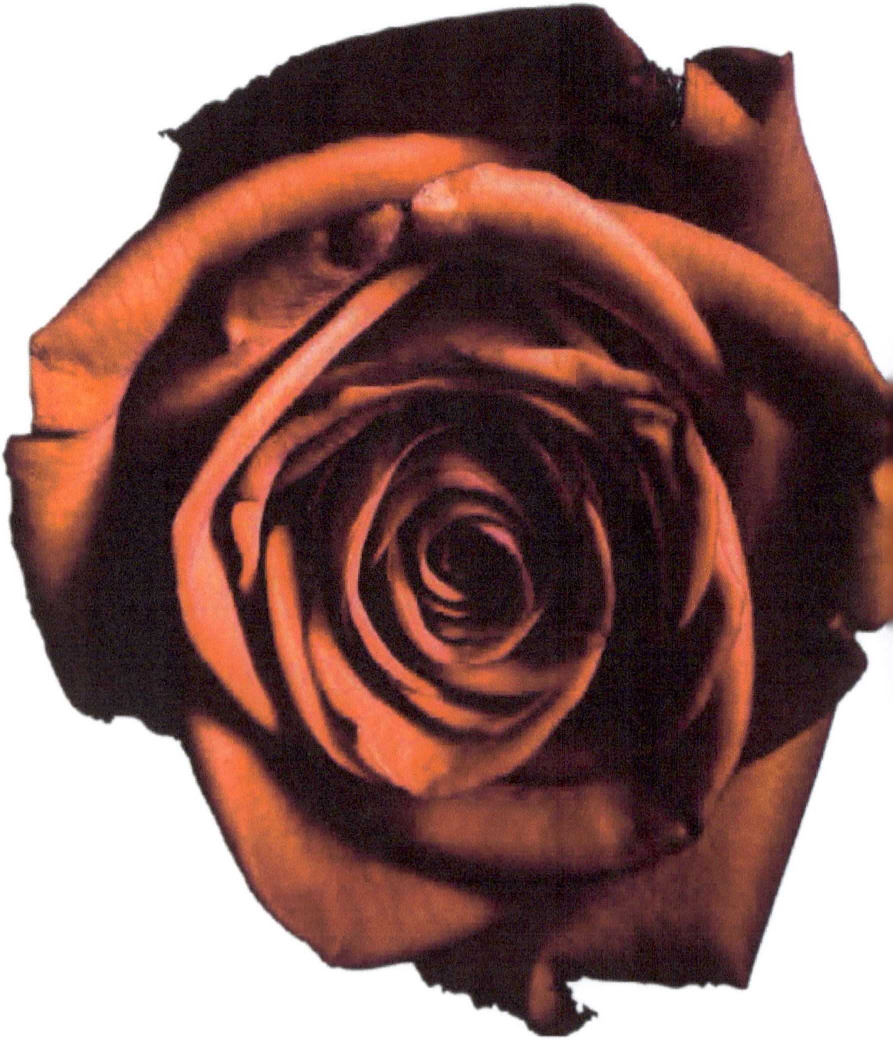

A Cry Answered (A Tribute to Oprah)

Today, the voices got to her
She heard the echoes, the cries of the children
Across the ocean
Across the desert
Across the wilderness
In her heart, she felt a pain, a pain of sadness
She is weakened, yet, enamored by voices she recalls
She wondered, "Is this my purpose?"
Tears roll down her face like fountain
water washes down a wall
Will the tears ever stop?

In the mirror, she saw a mother that she may never be
Behind the mirror, she saw a mother that she became
She recalled: Grandmother told her,
"Girl, one day, you will be somebody"
Now, her heart says, "Girl, go on and save somebody"
Her heart a beat too late because her mind was already there
She imagined the children, the lost dreams,
the lost souls, and the lost hope
She remembered the plea from a young African girl
The voice that never seizes to echo
The smile on her face that slowly vanished into
the shadows of darkness
She is overwhelmed by her mothering instinct
At this moment, can she control all her teardrops?

All these years of labor, hard work, and
pain left her the fruits of fulfillment
You see, deep down her soul, it comes natural
The endowment of God-instilled desire to save somebody
To lift the spirit, and to uproot the roots of poverty
She said to herself; "This is my calling"
Yes! The children of a painful world will be painless again
Oh! What a joyful world!
Jubilant chant echoes again
You can see happiness in their eyes when they say to her, "Thank you, Ma"
"Mama Africa," A name you deserved
You saved our lives
Here, she realizes the call is true
She looks at the mirror;
In soliloquy, she utters, "These are your own children"
This is your true calling.

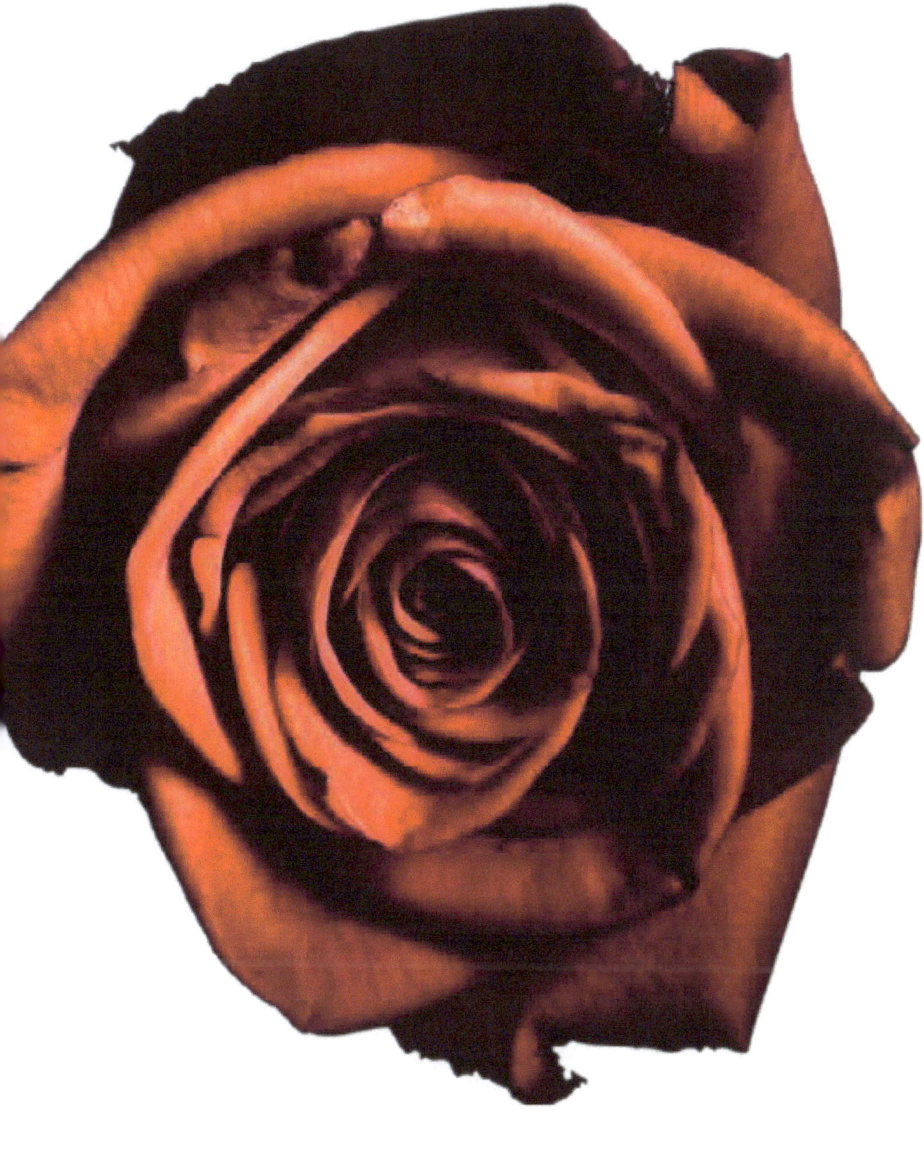

This Sunday Morning

Outside my bedroom window
A gloomy dark cloudy morning
Weary trees show premature fall colors
Not even August end, yet leaves are turning
August flowers display shriveled look
Where is the usual bright display of colors?
The elegant summer flowers seem to be absent
In replacement, the wet feel from the sluggish raindrops

I watch the raindrops knock down the leaves off the trees
Restless wind this summer calm this Sunday morning
This summer, the storm showed its face like a promise
A summer of destruction maybe a true reveal
of something coming
The trees, weary of the unusual summer storm,
let loose their leaves

This Sunday morning, the grass receives
the wet feel in satisfaction
But just yesterday, the heated atmosphere burnt
them in vengeance
The grass unappreciative, yet, happy to remain in perfection
But this Sunday morning, a relief
Truly the heat will return tomorrow in defiance
Wet grass once again will show a life of no significance

This Sunday morning, our world reveals a turning point
All Nature around us says we are in for new experiences
The destruction is near, but can we escape?

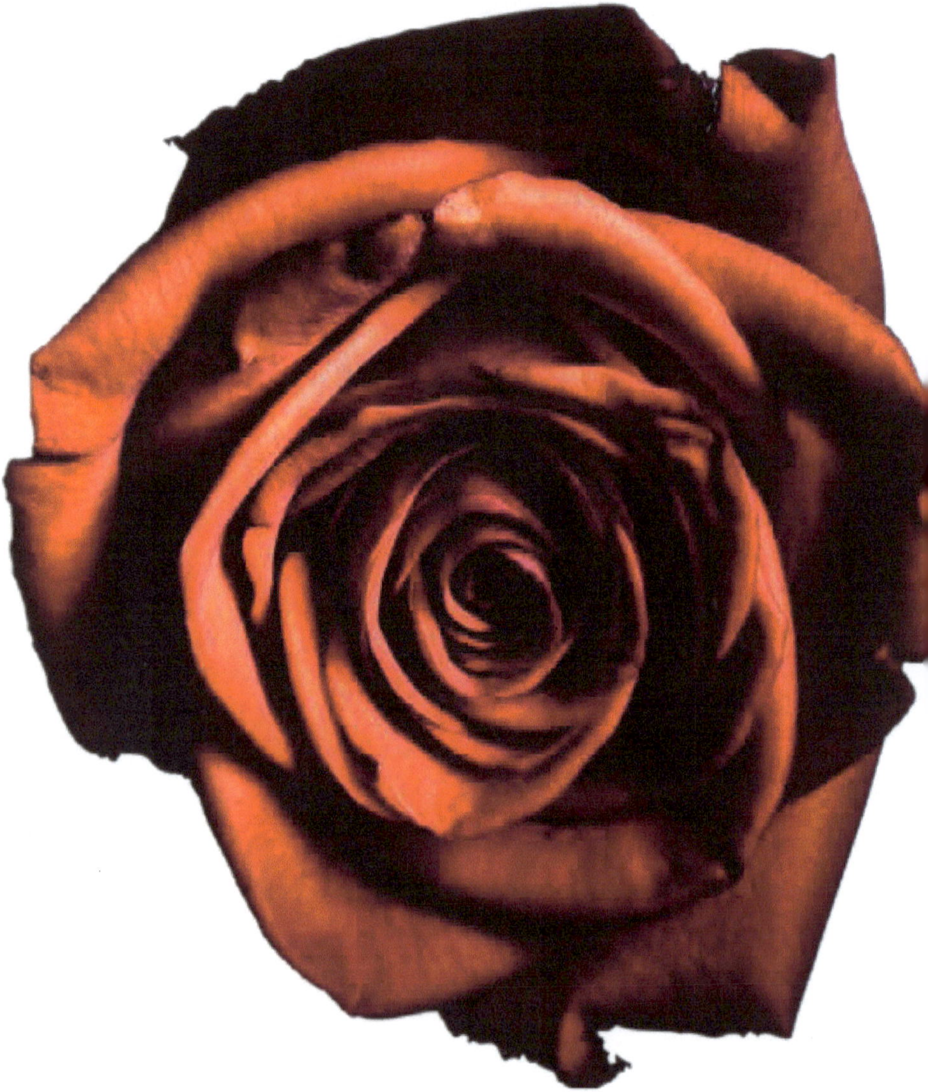

The Mid-Day Darkness

It's mid-day
My eyes; same eyes that just recovered
from the darkness of the night before
are already yearning for another darkness.
But, it's midday. The pale blue sky is beginning
to win a peek of expo-sure from the domineering clouds.

It's mid-day
The clouds in a majestic rhythmic motion
intending to leave behind the darkness of yesterday,
block the eye of the sun; the sun which now
has already planned on mounting an unrestricted
attack on our surface.

It's mid-day
While the earth's surface cries for attention,
the breeze of life directs attention to firm-rooted trees,
which now in a struggle to absorb the minerals of life
from the earth beneath.
They are beckoning for the sun, so as to let
loose the breath of life.
What a joy for the birds; clamoring and chattering
in feeding frenzy with great appreciation of Nature in motion!

The mid-day, once again, is laid to rest...
The sun?
The clouds of darkness have overcome,

and dusk has arrived ending the circle of Nature.
Me?
My eyes once more are shut
The mid-day is again darkness.

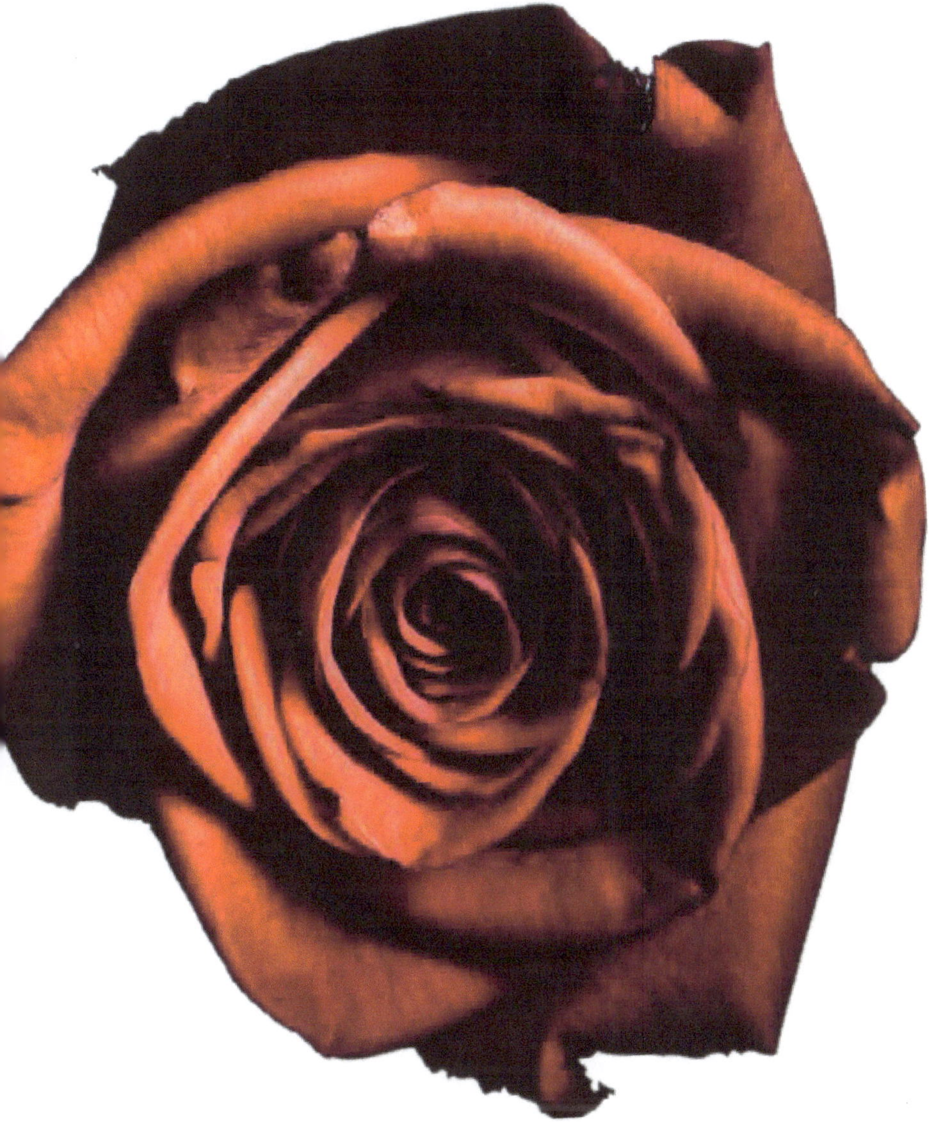

Without a Grudge

Sitting by the beachside, do you notice the quarrels?
Over there! The waves!
Their quarrels, their battles over the shoreline;
To be the first to reach the open sand.
Yet, the insignificant aquatic lives within, seem unaffected by the constant barrage and the collective unionized motion of the quarreling waves.
But once in a while, the sea lions, seals, and the penguins take advantage of the wave train transport, reaching the open sand, almost at the same time as the waves.
Do you think the waves would relent on a defeat or a tie race with the sea creatures?
The waves argued some more, and their quarrels continue as they push their way back into the sea, and again, out to the open sand.
Once again, transporting the aquatic creatures, still without a grudge.

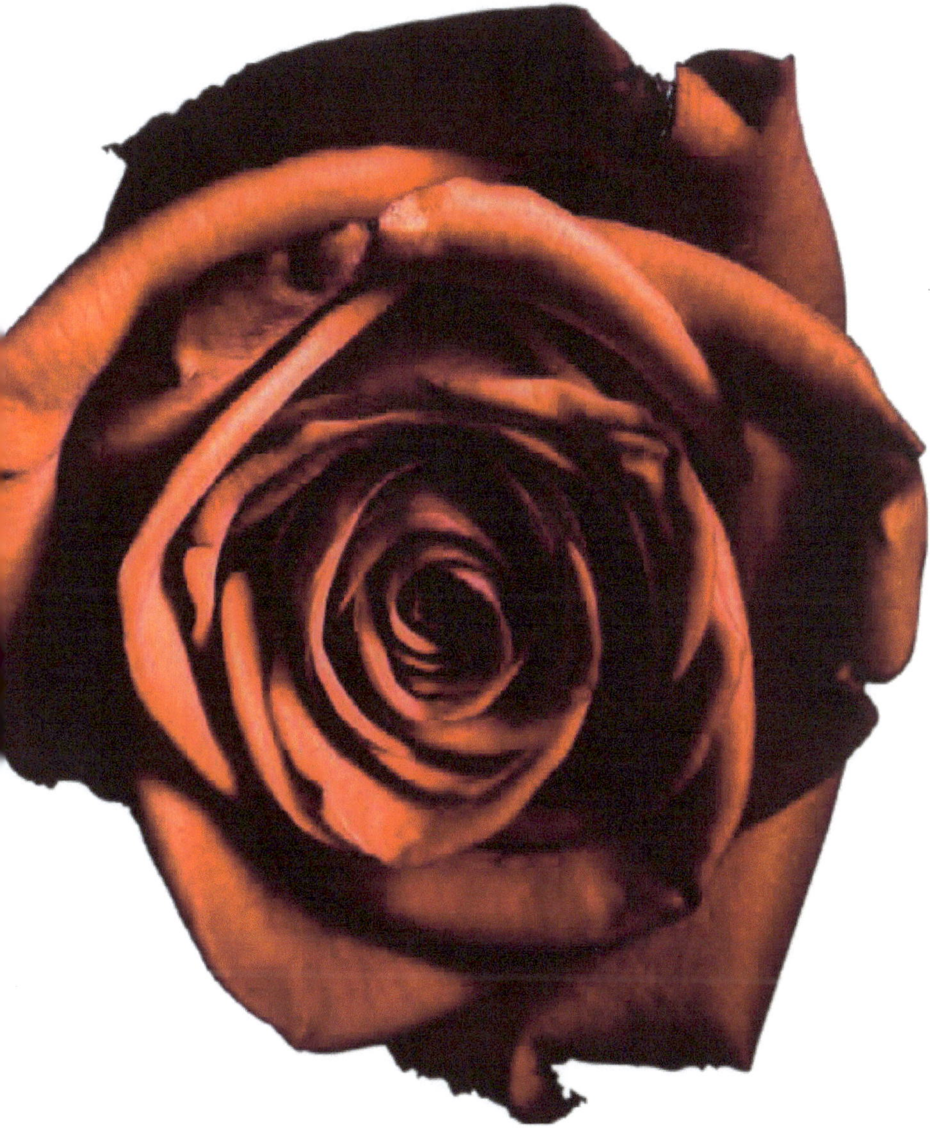

You Think You're Tired

Truly, the fatigue of life is here, but yes!
Too soon to say we are tired.
The face of the future seems clear;
Clear is the motivating description of the
future that brightens the cloud-ed reality.
Enchanting!
Sarcastically describes the corroded highway
into the endless dream of life that is full of compensations.
So, why do the good life and all these compensations
seem too far-fetched to be realized?
Oh yes! Choice!
Choice is the word.
No! Not personal choice!
You see…if that was a personal choice, the highway to
the future will be covered with smooth asphalt, and not
a single bump onsite.
But look! It is a choice that developed out of the desire
to succeed and excel. Now, these choices seem too rough
Too tough to conquer
That is why you think you are tired.

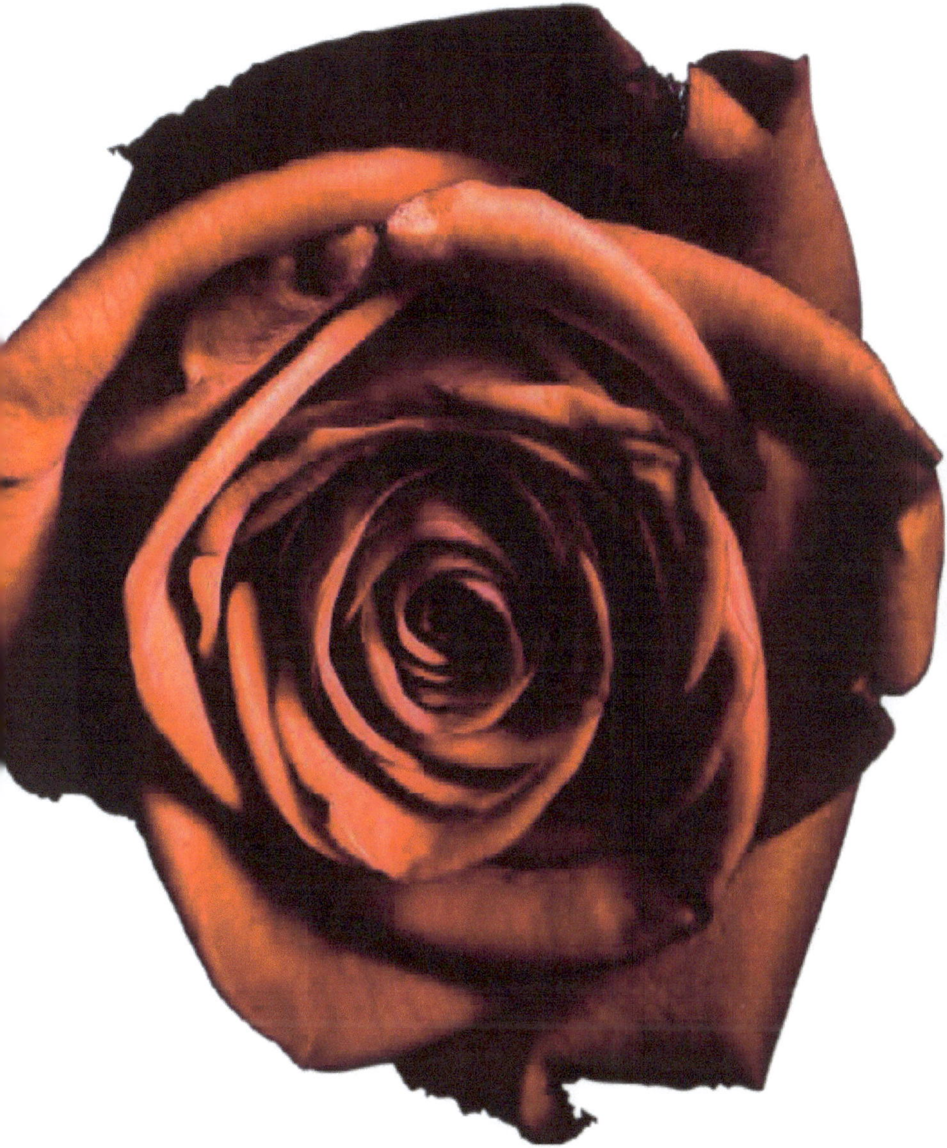

Here I Am

Now, here I am, for the destined purpose
The hustled and dazzled labor in vain
The promised fruits unreachable
The trials, tribulations, and struggles down the drain
Unexpected bumps become my landing strip too unstable

Here I am, fighting not to disappoint the gathering crowd
They will someday become the gathering acquaintances
Now, none seems to expect failure that looms overhead
The loot now disappears as it appeared at the onset
The beginning showed no image of stumble; only distance

My time strains and vanishes in the mist of misery amidst
Only my intuitions stay connected to the fishnet already cast
Here I am, holding on to the beginning thrust
Holding on to the only seed that is promising
Soon, the seed germinates, sure to sprout at a blink

Here I am, ripping what I sow
The fruits of labor that was meant to grow
Unwavering commitment on steady believe in intuition
Still, not enough to absolve the time taking in seclusion
I am reminded; faith remains questionable even for dreams assured.

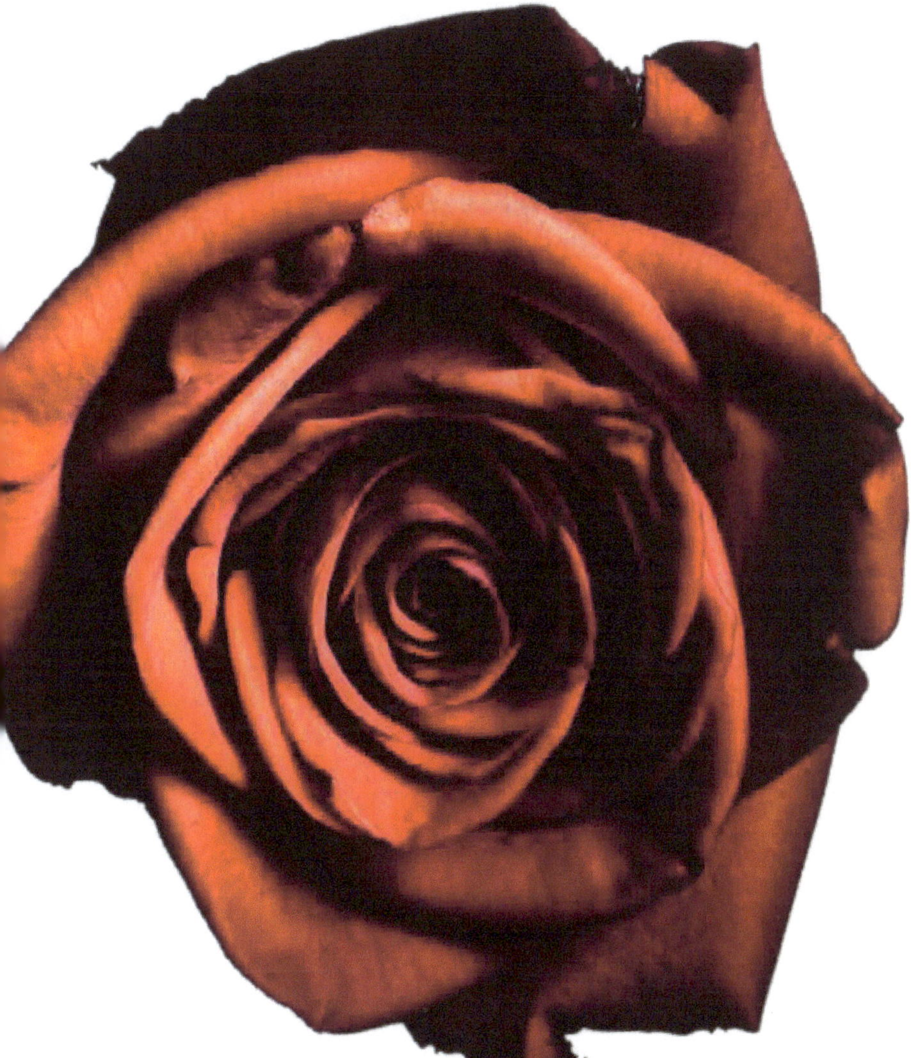

Frank's Life Quotes

Today's achievements are the results of
yesterday's visions of tomorrow.

And then, the King said,
Whence thou at my presence; Speak
But speak pleasant words, and bring good tidings.
Otherwise, hold thy tongue.

Bubble…
So precious
So delicate
So as friends and families
If so to it,
The world will fall into our hands
…As gentle as the bubble.

Life is nothing without a compromise
Your heart decides whom to love
But your mind holds you back
Let go of your mind
Love with no expectations
Then, accept love.

A clear mind will resolve your next
questionable sets of steps in life:
Sober up!

Realize that your trials in life are your
forward steps towards your destiny assured.

Wait for your time, as your clear horizon
appears to show your future:
No Rush!

Listen for your clarion call to answer
to your proposal to deal with life.

The road we follow in life has a crossroad
Eventually, we make the choice to follow
the road written for our fate

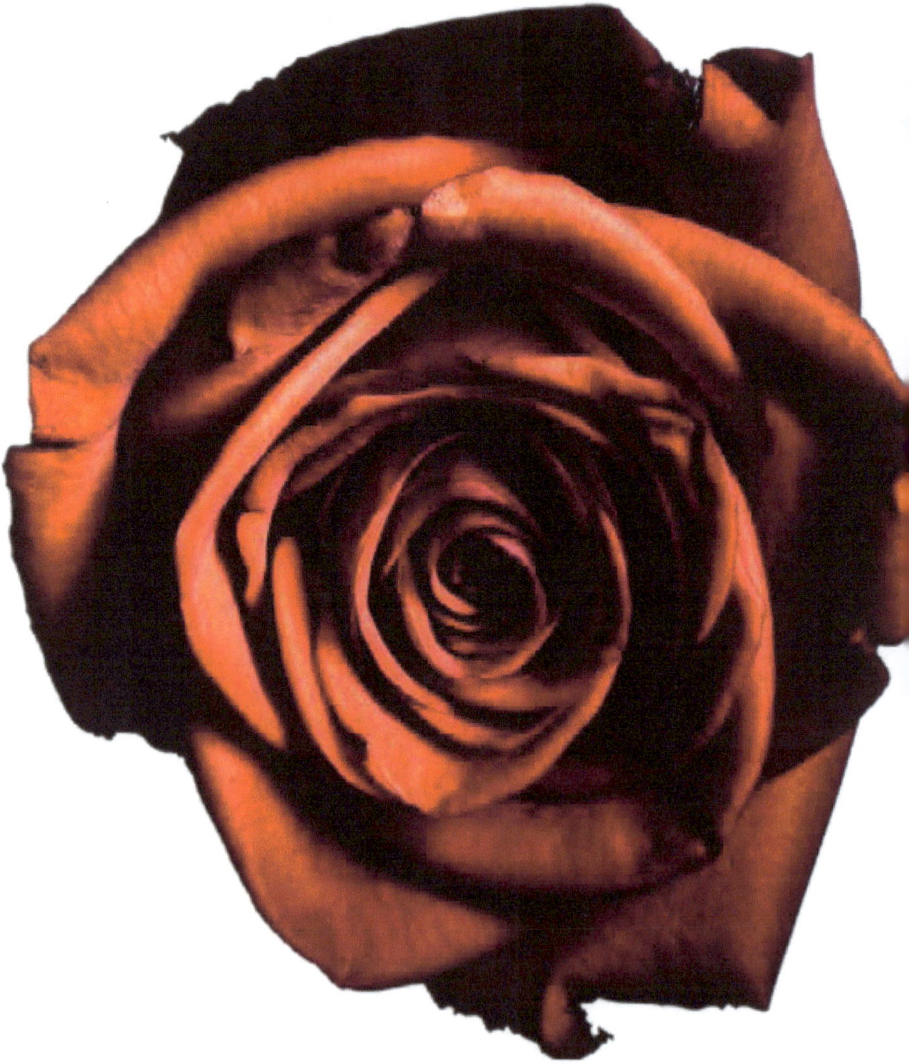

About the Author

Frank Chukwudubem Amobi, a father of one, was born on August 11, 1960, in the Northern part of Nigeria, Plateau, to the Late Honorable Sir, J.O.S. Amobi and Lady B.N. Amobi (nee Onubogu). He is the seventh of eight children. Frank migrated to the United States in 1981 where he obtained his bachelor's degree in political science at Howard University, Washington, D.C.

His first love has always been writing poems, screenplays, and then, music. He loves to play percussions, and also improvises piano jazz ballads. He lives in Maryland with his family.

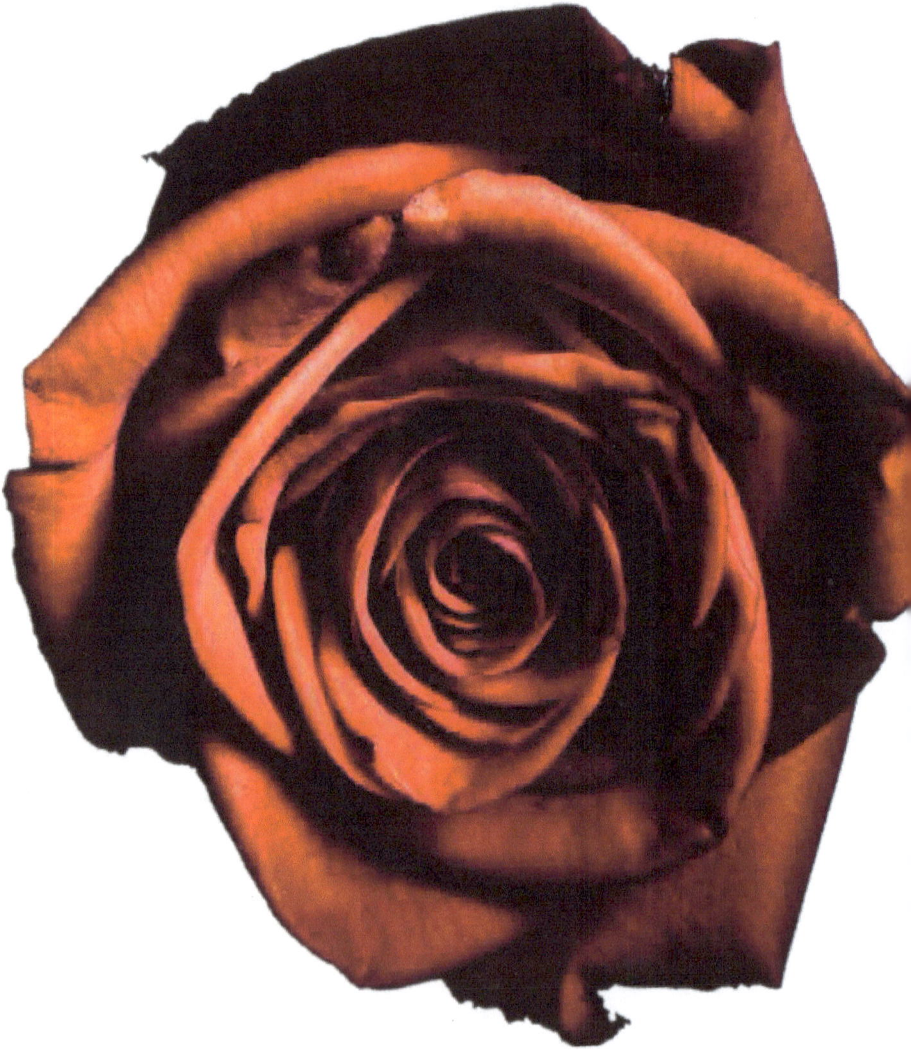